Kotlin 2.0 Crash Course

Build, test, and secure Android and web applications including Functional patterns, JSON handling, and RESTful endpoints

Elara Drevyn

Published by: GitforGits

Publisher: Sonal Dhandre

www.gitforgits.com

support@gitforgits.com

Printed in India

First Printing: Janurary 2025

ISBN: 978-93-49174-59-7

Cover Design by: Kitten Publishing

Prologue

From the very start of my professional journey, I have been amazed by how rapidly technology advances, and how frequently developers are compelled to master fresh tools without compromising their expertise. The latest version of Kotlin is packed with cutting-edge features, and it's incredible how much progress has been made. Many books on the subject could benefit from a bit of a speed boost. They tend to start off slow, going over basic syntax, and it takes them a while to dive into real-world applications. You're going to love this book! It's a fast-paced journey that covers every essential aspect of Kotlin 2.0. My goal is to present each topic so you can immediately apply it to a working sample project—no waiting until the end to see code come alive!

I built my own tooling and projects using Kotlin, and I saw that practitioners want both conceptual clarity and hands-on implementation without pages of dry theory. In "Kotlin 2.0 Crash Course," I speak directly to you, the developer who needs to solve problems today while laying a solid foundation for tomorrow. As you follow along, you'll learn how to install Kotlin on Linux, configure your development environment, and start writing code that compiles without hiccups. I'm thrilled to guide you through the fascinating world of variables, data types, and control structures. I'll use clear examples that immediately demonstrate how Task Tracker stores and manipulates tasks.

Next, I'm thrilled to introduce functions, where you'll discover how to avoid repetitive code by writing reusable helpers, embracing lambdas, and leveraging higher-order patterns. We're thrilled to dive into object-oriented constructs, where you'll witness the incredible power of classes and constructors as they beautifully model real entities. With interfaces and inheritance, we'll explore the amazing way they streamline our work, reducing duplication and enhancing efficiency. I'm thrilled to explain access modifiers and encapsulation so you can maintain strong boundaries between your core logic and external components. I'm thrilled to share the details of collection handling, which showcases the incredible power of lists, arrays, sets, and maps. These essential tools become the foundation for storing, filtering, and traversing data in your applications.

And the best part is that state management receives special attention because real applications must respond to user actions, background processes, and asynchronous events. I'm thrilled to show you how to blend immutable snapshots with mutable references and use observer patterns to keep every component in sync. And then, we'll dive into the exciting world of functional programming with lambdas! You'll learn to chain operations, compose transformations, and write declarative data pipelines that replace boilerplate loops.

There's nothing more critical than handling errors, and I devote a whole chapter to the most effective techniques: try-catch patterns, safe casts, and centralized logging. You'll learn how to catch exceptions early, log them consistently, and recover from failures without crashing. Once we dive into JSON serialization, I'll guide you on how to parse and encode data using Kotlinx.serialization, Moshi, or Jackson, and how to map nested JSON structures into Kotlin types.

After that, I'll guide you through the exciting world of RESTful API design, where I'll reveal how resource-oriented URIs, HTTP methods, and versioning team up to deliver endpoints that you can count on. You'll build incredible endpoints that will allow you to create, read, update, and delete tasks with ease. And you'll learn to integrate with a database via Exposed and H2 — sounds exciting, right? By the time you reach chapter twelve, you'll be ready to dive into the exciting world of Ktor server setup, defining routes, and installing middleware for logging and validation. And of course, you'll be testing every component systematically, ensuring everything is up to par.

With this book, I'm making a single, streamlined path from zero to a production-ready Kotlin application. Prepare to be amazed, because you won't find unrelated detours here! Instead, you'll see an exciting, focused progression of chapters, each building on what came before, all tied to a practical Task Tracker project. I wrote every sentence as if I were sitting beside you, pointing out key details and common pitfalls. By the time you finish, you'll have not only a solid understanding of Kotlin 2.0 but also a real, working web and Android-capable service that you can extend, customize, and deploy!

Content

Preface

If you're looking to write responsive Android and web applications using Kotlin 2.0, this book's got you covered with some great examples. The book starts by showing you how to install Kotlin 2.0 on Linux and configure IntelliJ IDEA so that your Task Tracker project compiles and runs without hiccups. In the early chapters, you'll dive into the basics of variables, data types, and control structures like if-else, when, while, and do-while. This'll lay a solid foundation of logic, while also giving you hands-on experience storing and manipulating task entries.

There's a chapter on functions that'll teach you to write reusable code, use higher-order functions, and adopt lambda expressions to streamline operations in the project. As you move into object-oriented constructs, you'll learn to define classes, primary and secondary constructors, inheritance, interfaces, and encapsulation practices that keep internal task details safe and modular. Then, we'll dive into collection handling, where we'll use lists, arrays, sets, and maps along with some handy code that'll filter, transform, and iterate through tasks like a pro.

In the state management section, you'll see how immutable snapshots and mutable services work together using observers to sync components in real time. The chapters on functional programming will walk you through chaining, mapping, and flattening data pipelines. This replaces manual loops with concise, expressive code. The error handling and type casting chapters will show you how to catch and log exceptions, apply safe casts, and recover from unexpected conditions without crashing.

If one wants to get really into JSON serialization, it's possible to learn how to parse JSON into Kotlin objects, serialize tasks back into JSON, and use libraries like kotlinx.serialization or Moshi for nested structures. In the RESTful API design segment, you'll learn about resource-oriented endpoints, HTTP methods, versioning, and content negotiation. Finally, Ktor integration teaches you to initialize a coroutine-based server, define routes, install middleware, secure endpoints with authentication, and test your components thoroughly.

This book won't turn you into a Kotlin master overnight, but it'll give you the confidence and hands-on experience you need to build real-world Android and web apps with Kotlin 2.0 right from the start.

In this book we will learn to:

- Build strong foundation in Kotlin 2.0 syntax to write clear, concise code.
- Absorb strong designing principles including classes, constructors, inheritance, and encapsulation for robust design.
- Gain practical mastery in using lists, arrays, sets, and maps to store, filter, and transform the data efficiently.

- AStrong hold on coroutine-based state management and observer patterns for responsive, synchronized application behavior.
- Develop fluency in functional programming alongwith lambdas to process data pipelines succinctly.
- Manage error handling and safe casts, ensuring your application recovers gracefully from runtime issues.
- Perform JSON parsing and serialization using kotlinx.serialization, Moshi, and Jackson.
- Practical implementation of Ktor's routing, plugins, middleware, and testing for web server development.
- Streamlined testing and debugging workflow, combining in-memory tests, logging, and profiling to catch issues.

GitforGits

Prerequisites

This book is a fast-paced practical learning for developers, programmers, application engineers who demands a fast learning and that too practical touchbase to every aspect of Kotlin that can be put into use. Prior knowledge of object oriented programming is all you need to begin with this book.

Codes Usage

Are we in need of some helpful code examples to assist we in our programming and documentation? Look no further! Our book offers a wealth of supplemental material, including code examples and exercises.

Not only is this book here to aid we in getting our job done, but we have our permission to use the example code in our programs and documentation. However, please note that if we are reproducing a significant portion of the code, we do require we to contact us for permission.

But don't worry, using several chunks of code from this book in our program or answering a question by citing our book and quoting example code does not require permission. But if we do choose to give credit, an attribution typically includes the title, author, publisher, and ISBN. For example, "Kotlin 2.0 Crash Course by Elara Drevyn".

If we are unsure whether our intended use of the code examples falls under fair use or the permissions outlined above, please do not hesitate to reach out to us at support@gitforgits.com.

We are happy to assist and clarify any concerns.

Acknowledgement

I owe a tremendous debt of gratitude to GitforGits, for their unflagging enthusiasm and wise counsel throughout the entire process of writing this book. Their knowledge and careful editing helped make sure the piece was useful for people of all reading levels and comprehension skills. In addition, I'd like to thank everyone involved in the publishing process for their efforts in making this book a reality. Their efforts, from copyediting to advertising, made the project what it is today.

Finally, I'd like to express my gratitude to everyone who has shown me unconditional love and encouragement throughout my life. Their support was crucial to the completion of this book. I appreciate our help with this endeavour and our continued interest in my career.

CHAPTER 1: UP AND RUNNING WITH KOTLIN 2.0

Chapter Overview

We'll start by taking a look at why Kotlin 2.0 has become so important in modern development. First, we will start with its roots at JetBrains, then see how it made its way into Android, and finally, how big companies like Pinterest and Uber used it to great success. Then, we will see how features like null-safety, coroutines, and concise syntax really shine in the real world.

We then get our Linux workstation ready for Kotlin development, starting with installing the OpenJDK `17, set up SDKMAN to handle the Kotlin `2.0.20 compiler, and then making sure our environment can reliably compile and run Kotlin code. Once you've set up the environment, we will need to configure IntelliJ IDEA Community Edition as our main development hub. We will be integrating essential plugins like Gradle Kotlin DSL support for building scripts, EditorConfig for consistent styling, Detekt and Ktlint for static analysis and formatting, and optional tools like Arrow Meta and Swagger/OpenAPI for advanced metaprogramming and API documentation. For each plugin installation, we'll walk we through the process step-by-step, and we will get to confirm that everything's working by importing and running the TaskTracker starter project.

After all the necessary tools in place, we will dive into Kotlin 2.0's modern syntax enhancements. We will apply context-receivers to get rid of repetitive parameters, define value classes to model domain types without runtime cost, and refactor our REPL loop to use sealed interfaces and exhaustive when-expressions. We will use contracts to improve flow analysis and adopt new standard library extensions for collection transformations. Throughout, we will be refactoring the Task Tracker code base as it happens, and we will see how each improvement makes the code cleaner, safer, and easier to maintain.

Kotlin 2.0 Overview

You may recall when Java reigned supreme on the JVM, yet verbose syntax and null-pointer pitfalls often slowed we down. In 2011, JetBrains introduced a new language that aimed to streamline code and eliminate common errors. By 2017, Google gave Kotlin first-class status for Android development, and a surge of adoption followed. We might observe that, today, more than half of active Android projects include Kotlin code. Companies such as Pinterest reported a 20 percent drop in crash rates after migrating key modules to Kotlin, thanks to null-safety and improved type inference. Uber moved core microservices to Kotlin coroutines, achieving 15 percent lower latency under peak loads. These successes demonstrate how Kotlin's features deliver tangible improvements in developer productivity, stability, and performance.

What makes Kotlin 2.0 Different?

We now stand at the threshold of Kotlin 2.0—a release focused on expressiveness, safety, and speed. We will see context-receivers that let us write domain-specific languages with minimal ceremony, so our code reads more like natural instructions than boilerplate. We will benefit from value classes, which model domain concepts without the runtime overhead of object allocation. We will notice faster compile times—up to 30 percent improvements on large codebases in JetBrains benchmarks—so our feedback loop stays tight. We will encounter stronger flow analysis that catches more logic errors at compile time, sparing we from elusive bugs later on. Such enhancements move Kotlin beyond a Java replacement toward a multi-paradigm tool for Android, server-side, web, and native development.

Following features makes Kotlin Outstanding:

1. Android Apps with Null-Safety

We build an app that processes user-generated content. Kotlin's type system ensures that nullable data is handled explicitly, preventing unexpected crashes when network responses omit fields. Pinterest saw crash-rate reductions by enforcing non-null properties in critical view models.

2. High-Throughput Microservices

We design services that handle thousands of requests per second. Kotlin coroutines let us write asynchronous code in a sequential style, avoiding thread-blocking and boosting throughput. Uber reported 15 percent lower latency after rewriting Java threads as coroutines.

3. Domain-Specific Languages (DSLs)

We create a configuration DSL for build scripts or UI layouts. Context-receivers in Kotlin 2.0 remove repetitive qualifiers, making our DSL concise and self-documenting. Teams at Gradle have explored Kotlin DSL improvements to simplify build configuration.

4. Cross-Platform Projects

We share business logic between Android, iOS, and web clients. Kotlin Multiplatform compiles common code into JVM, JavaScript, and native binaries. We maintain one codebase for validation rules, data models, and algorithms, reducing duplication and ensuring consistency.

Introducing Task Tracker Sample Project

We will use Kotlin 2.0 to our simple command-line Task Tracker project. At first, it supports adding, listing, and removing tasks in memory. We follow along, writing basic Kotlin constructs—variables, control flow, and functions—to manage tasks. As chapters progress, we integrate value classes for **`TaskId`** and **`TaskDescription`**, ensuring type safety without performance penalties. We will adopt context-receivers to separate command parsing from business logic, yielding a neat, domain-specific API for new commands. When we add JSON serialization, Kotlin 2.0 contracts guarantee exhaustive handling of data models. Later, coroutines empower non-blocking periodic reminders or network-backed persistence. Finally, we'll build a Ktor-based HTTP server that exposes RESTful endpoints for remote task management.

How Kotlin 2.0 elevates our app?

Feature	**Benefit to Task Tracker**
Value Classes	Represent **`TaskId`** without runtime overhead, enforcing type safety.
Context-Receivers	Cleanly inject shared dependencies (parsers, loggers) into commands.
Faster Compilation	Shorten development cycles as we iterate on Task Tracker features.
Enhanced Flow Analysis	Catch missing **`when`** branches on task statuses at compile time.
Coroutines	Introduce non-blocking reminders or persistence without thread hacks.

You define

```
@JvmInline value class TaskId(val id: UUID)
```

so that our compiler treats **`TaskId`** as a simple **`UUID`** at runtime. No extra objects, no boxing overhead—yet the type system prevents us from mixing up IDs with descriptions.

Let us imagine a command handler:

```
context(CommandParser, TaskService)
fun addTask(description: String) { … }
```

With this, we no longer pass parser and service instances manually. The compiler understands context, yielding code that reads like plain English: "with parser and service, perform addTask."

Also, when we tweak the JSON format or adjust a coroutine timeout, compile times remain snappy. We spend less time waiting and more time coding, testing, and refining.

Let us sat engage ourselves with our project right away. We can simply begin by cloning the starter repo, opening it in our IDE, and running the bare-bones Task Tracker with commands like:

```
> add "Write chapter on Kotlin overview"
```

```
> list
1: Write chapter on Kotlin overview
> remove 1
```

This immediate feedback cements our understanding of Kotlin's REPL-style execution. As we progress through Chapter 1, we will refactor the main loop to use **`when`** expressions, inline functions, and enhanced data types.

Installing Kotlin Toolkit and Dependencies

We will begin by readying our Ubuntu system for Kotlin development. Keeping our operating system current prevents unexpected errors when installing new software. Open a terminal and type **`sudo apt update && sudo apt upgrade -y`** to fetch the latest package information and apply security fixes. This single command ensures our system libraries and package indexes remain aligned with upstream repositories. While that runs, consider how a stable base enables us to focus on coding rather than troubleshooting mismatched dependencies. When the process finishes, our machine stands prepared to host the Java Development Kit, the Kotlin compiler, and IntelliJ IDEA—the trio we need to breathe life into the Task Tracker sample project.

Installing JDK

Kotlin targets the Java Virtual Machine, so a modern JDK must be in place. We install the default JDK provided by Ubuntu, which typically maps to OpenJDK 17 or later—perfectly compatible with Kotlin 2.0.

We simply type:

```
sudo apt install default-jdk -y
```

When the prompt returns, we then verify by:

```
java -version
```

You can expect an output similar to:

```
openjdk version "17.0.x" …
```

This confirms that our JVM is ready to execute Kotlin bytecode and that the Kotlin compiler can generate class files targeting a supported Java version DigitalOceanAsk Ubuntu.

Managing Kotlin Versions with SDKMAN!

Now here, to keep the Kotlin compiler aligned with our examples, we employ SDKMAN!, a version manager for JVM-based tools. It installs, switches, and updates SDKs without manual path juggling.

To do this, we run:

```
curl -s "https://get.sdkman.io" | bash
source "$HOME/.sdkman/bin/sdkman-init.sh"
```

The SDKMAN! initializes itself in our shell. We can confirm by typing **sdk version**. To install Kotlin 2.0.20—the exact release used in our Task Tracker examples—enter:

```
sdk install kotlin 2.0.20
```

When prompted to set it as default, type **Y**. Finally, check the compiler version:

```
kotlinc -version
```

You should be able to see:

```
info: kotlinc-jvm 2.0.20
```

With this, our environment consistently invokes Kotlin 2.0.20, matching every code snippet and ensuring reproducible results Kotlin.

Exploring Environment Variables

The SDKMAN! places the Kotlin binaries under the following path:

~/.sdkman/candidates/kotlin/current/bin

Here, our shell's **PATH** is updated automatically when SDKMAN! initializes. If we ever face a "command not found" error for **kotlinc** or **kotlin**, add the following lines to our **~/.bashrc** or **~/.zshrc**:

```
export SDKMAN_DIR="$HOME/.sdkman"
source "$SDKMAN_DIR/bin/sdkman-init.sh"
```

After this, save and reload our shell with **source ~/.bashrc** (or **source ~/.zshrc**). This guarantees that each new terminal session locates the Kotlin compiler, so we never lose precious coding time chasing missing executables.

Installing IntelliJ IDEA Community Edition via Snap

You'll be crafting, compiling, and debugging Kotlin code inside IntelliJ IDEA, which is known for its deep Kotlin integration. If you're into simplicity, you'll love how easy it is to install and update with Snap.

```
sudo snap install intellij-idea-community --classic
```

The **`--classic`** flag grants IntelliJ full system access akin to a traditional package. After installation, launch with **`intellij-idea-community`**. On first run, accept default settings or import any existing preferences. IntelliJ bundles a Kotlin plugin compatible with version 2.0.20, so no manual plugin updates are required Snapcraft.

Configuring IntelliJ

When IntelliJ opens, first select ***New Project*** › ***Kotlin*** › ***JVM | IDEA***. In the build-system step choose ***Gradle*** with the ***Kotlin/JVM*** DSL. Set ***Kotlin version*** to **`2.0.20`**. Our generated **`build.gradle.kts`** will include:

```
plugins {
    kotlin("jvm") version "2.0.20"
}
repositories {
    mavenCentral()
}
dependencies {
    implementation(kotlin("stdlib"))
}
```

After this, click ***Finish***. The IntelliJ automatically syncs the Gradle project. You can watch the ***Event Log*** at the bottom right; a successful import appears within seconds. With this, we now have an IDE project configured to compile against Kotlin 2.0.20 and target the standard library.

Importing Task Tracker Starter Code

To do this, within IntelliJ, choose ***File*** › ***Open***, then navigate to the unzipped **`TaskTracker`** folder. The IntelliJ detects the Gradle build and prompts to import. Just click agree and let the IDE index all files. In the ***Gradle*** panel, expand ***Tasks*** › ***application*** and double-click ***run***. The Run console displays:

```
> list
No tasks found.
> add "Initialize environment"
Task added: 1
```

This immediate feedback loop shows the minimal starter in action, confirming that our environment, compiler, and IDE are correctly aligned.

Examining Project Structure

Now if you look in the Project tool window, you'll see:

```
TaskTracker/
├── build.gradle.kts
├── settings.gradle.kts
├── gradlew, gradlew.bat, gradle/
└── src/
    └── main/
        └── kotlin/
            └── tracker/
                └── Main.kt
```

Here, you open **`Main.kt`** to see the simple REPL loop that reads commands, matches them using **`when`**, and manipulates an in-memory list of tasks. We will enhance this file immediately in the next topic. Because Kotlin 2.0 compiles quickly on modern hardware—often in under a second for small changes—every edit we make will be validated almost instantly.

Troubleshooting Common Issues

If **`kotlinc`** reports an unexpected version, we simply double-check **`sdk current kotlin`**. If IntelliJ fails to sync Gradle, open the ***Build*** tool window and click ***Refresh all Gradle projects***. For Snap-related permission errors, run **`sudo snap connect intellij-idea-community:...`** as suggested in the error message. Should we encounter a missing JDK error inside the IDE, confirm that ***Project SDK*** under ***File*** › ***Project Structure*** points to the system's Java 17 installation.

With JDK, Kotlin 2.0.20, SDKMAN!, and IntelliJ IDEA operational, our Linux workstation has transformed into a Kotlin playground. We see the Task Tracker prompt in our Run console; we can edit **`Main.kt`**, press ***Ctrl + Shift + F10***, and observe the updated behavior. This instant gratification cements the link between code and outcome, fueling our motivation to explore Kotlin's modern features. In the next topic—Variables, Data Types, and Basic Operations—you will declare typed properties in **`Main.kt`**, replace raw strings with value classes, and witness how

Kotlin's type system assists us toward safer, more maintainable code.

Configuring IDE

We have a working Kotlin 2.0.20 compiler and IntelliJ IDEA Community Edition. Now we enhance our workflow by adding plugins that streamline coding, enforce best practices, and accelerate debugging. Each plugin we install becomes a teammate: one suggests code completions, another highlights performance pitfalls, a third formats our code to a consistent style. As we build the Task Tracker, these plugins catch errors before they happen, document our APIs automatically, and integrate testing tools so we can verify new features within seconds.

Kotlin Plugin

The IntelliJ bundles the Kotlin plugin, which provides syntax highlighting, code completion, refactorings, and immediate inspections for Kotlin code. We already saw how IntelliJ recognized **`build.gradle.kts`** and offered to import. That functionality comes from this plugin.

Now, how to verify? Well, in IntelliJ's main menu, choose ***File* › *Settings* › *Plugins***. Under the ***Installed*** tab, search for "Kotlin." We should see "Kotlin" marked as Enabled. Its version matches our IDE build, and it ensures full support for Kotlin 2.0.20 source files. No further action is required here, but knowing it is active gives confidence that every Kotlin construct—whether a value class or context-receiver—receives correct editor support.

Gradle Kotlin DSL Support

When we author **`build.gradle.kts`**, this plugin supplies code completion, type-checking, and quick navigation for Gradle's Kotlin DSL. We can import dependencies, configure tasks, and refactor build logic with the same tooling advantages us enjoy in application code.

How to install?

- In Settings › Plugins, click the Marketplace tab.
- Search for "Gradle Kotlin DSL."
- Click Install, then Restart IDE when prompted.

First, open the **`build.gradle.kts`** and begin typing **`kotlin("jvm") version`**. The IDE suggests completions, shows available versions, and flags mistakes such as missing parentheses. As we add plugins for serialization or Ktor, autocompletion ensures our Gradle script remains correct and up to date.

.editorconfig Support

An **`.editorconfig`** file at the project root defines indentation, line endings, naming conventions, and more. The plugin applies these rules automatically as we type or reformat.

To install:

- In ***Settings*** › ***Plugins***, search "EditorConfig."
- Install and restart.

At our project root, just create a file named **`.editorconfig`** and add rules:

```
root = true
[*.{kt,kts}]
indent_style = space
indent_size = 4
continuation_indent_size = 8
insert_final_newline = true
max_line_length = 120
charset = utf-8
```

After this, the IntelliJ highlights any deviation from these rules. When we press ***Ctrl + Alt + L*** (Reformat Code), our Kotlin files conform automatically.

Arrow Meta

The Arrow Meta brings meta-programming capabilities to Kotlin. We can define custom compiler plugins, lint rules, or DSL transforms. For the Task Tracker, we might use Arrow Meta later to generate boilerplate for command handlers or to enforce that every **`when`** expression over task statuses remains exhaustive.

To install:

- In ***Settings*** › ***Plugins***, search "Arrow Meta."
- Install and restart.

To put into use, just add the following to our Gradle build:

```
plugins {
  id("arrow.meta") version "1.3.2"
}
```

Then write a simple lint rule in **`src/main/kotlin`** that flags any non-exhaustive **`when`** on our **`TaskStatus`** sealed class. We see warnings in the editor before we compile. This proactive feedback guards against logic holes.

RESTful Toolkit / Swagger UI Integration

When we begin defining REST endpoints in Ktor, this plugin assists by generating OpenAPI (Swagger) specifications and embedding an interactive UI. We can test CRUD operations on our Task Tracker API without leaving the IDE.

To install, search "Swagger" or "OpenAPI." Now to use, add the OpenAPI feature in our Ktor module:

```
install(OpenAPIGen) {
  swagger {
    forwardRoot = true
  }
}
```

Then just reload the project. Then, in IntelliJ's HTTP client or embedded browser, navigate to `http://localhost:8080/swagger-ui`. You will see our Task Tracker endpoints documented and can exercise them with sample JSON bodies.

Code Quality and Linting Plugins

Detekt

It is a static code analysis for Kotlin. It finds complexity hotspots, unused code, potential bugs, style violations, and security issues.

Simply search for "Detekt.", install it and restart. Now to integrate, write the following in **`build.gradle.kts`**:

```
plugins {
  id("io.gitlab.arturbosch.detekt") version "1.21.0"
}
detekt {
  config = files("$rootDir/detekt-config.yml")
  buildUponDefaultConfig = true
}
```

Then run **`./gradlew detekt`** to generate an HTML report. In IntelliJ, the Detekt tool window highlights issues inline. We will run this after adding new modules to ensure code quality remains high.

Ktlint

This one enforces Kotlin style guide. It automatically formats code on save or commit. Just install as you did the previous ones and then to integrate, write the following in **build.gradle.kts**:

```
plugins {
  id("org.jlleitschuh.gradle.ktlint") version "11.0.0"
}
ktlint {
  version.set("0.48.2")
  enableExperimentalRules.set(true)
}
```

After this, the **./gradlew ktlintFormat** automatically reformats code. We can add a pre-commit hook so every **git commit** triggers **ktlintCheck** and **ktlintFormat**.

Database and Serialization Helpers

When we add JSON serialization and later integrate a lightweight embedded database (e.g. H2 or SQLite), these plugins help as below:

- ***SQL Delight*** – generates typesafe Kotlin APIs from SQL statements.
- ***Kotlinx Serialization*** – assists in JSON, ProtoBuf, and CBOR serialization.

To integrate, just install it as we did the other plugind and then to integrate, write the following in **build.gradle.kts**:

```
plugins {
  id("com.squareup.sqldelight") version "1.5.4"
  kotlin("plugin.serialization") version "2.0.20"
}
sqldelight {
  database("TaskDatabase") {
    packageName = "tracker.db"
  }
}
```

```
dependencies {
  implementation("org.jetbrains.kotlinx:kotlinx-serialization-json:1.6.0")
  implementation("com.squareup.sqldelight:sqlite-driver:1.5.4")
}
```

This will define our **`tasks.sq`** file under **`src/main/sqldelight/tracker/db`**, and SQL Delight generates a **`TaskDatabase`** API we call from service classes. After installing and configuring each of the above plugins, go to ***File › Invalidate Caches / Restart***, choose ***Invalidate and Restart***.

Once IntelliJ restarts, open the ***Event Log*** and ***Problems*** tool windows to confirm no plugin errors appear. Now in ***Gradle*** pane, trigger a full rebuild:

```
./gradlew clean build
```

In ***Run*** console, re-execute the Task Tracker:

```
./gradlew run
```

Now here, we have to ensure that the commands still function as before:

```
> add "Verify plugins"
Task added: 1
> list
1: Verify plugins
```

By doing this, we've turned IntelliJ IDEA into a super powerful Kotlin 2.0 tool. Every code sample after this one—whether it's a LINQ-style collection filter, an inline lambda callback, or a Ktor routing block—will get real-time feedback, automated formatting, and static analysis. Now, we're all set to dive into the heart of Kotlin syntax, knowing our IDE will support every keystroke, spot every misstep, and help us build a solid Task Tracker application.

Modern Kotlin Syntax and Enhancements

We know you've worked with Kotlin in the past, but we know that there have still been times when boilerplate or awkward constructs have gotten in your way. Kotlin 2.0 has some cool new features. It gets rid of ceremony, makes sure things are more reliable when you compile, and makes it easier to show what you mean. As we continue to improve the Task Tracker, these changes will make refactoring smoother and every new feature more concise. We'll see how context-receivers get rid of repetitive parameters, how value classes model domain types without overhead, and how upgraded **when** expressions, contracts, and standard-library extensions reduce friction in everyday coding. By when we're done with this topic, we'll see why Kotlin 2.0 seems more like expressive prose than traditional code.

Context-Receivers

In earlier Kotlin versions, we passed shared services or utilities into every function that needed them. Our **addTask** function might look like:

```
fun addTask(parser: CommandParser, service: TaskService,
input: String) {
    val description = parser.parse(input)
    service.createTask(description)
}
```

You found yourself threading **parser** and **service** through multiple layers.

One most important thing isd that, the Context-receivers let us declare that certain types are available in the function's context, without explicit parameters:

```
context(CommandParser, TaskService)
fun addTask(input: String) {
    val description = parse(input)       // parser.parse under
the hood
    createTask(description)              // service.createTask
implicitly
}
```

The compiler injects **this@CommandParser** and **this@TaskService** so we can call their members directly.

Now, to apply to our appl, we need to first open **Main.kt** and locate the command-dispatch section. Here, we need to replace the existing signature:

```
fun handleAdd(parser: CommandParser, service: TaskService,
args: String) { … }
```

with:

```
context(CommandParser, TaskService)
fun handleAdd(args: String) {
    val description = parse(args)
    val id = createTask(description)
    println("Task added: $id")
}
```

In our REPL loop, call it like:

```
with(parser, service) { handleAdd(input) }
```

After this, you remove parameter clutter, and our code reads as if we wrote a mini-DSL: "with parser and service, handleAdd."

Value Classes

The representation of a task's identifier as a **String** or **UUID** works, but we risk mixing IDs with other strings accidentally. The Kotlin 2.0's **@JvmInline value class** wraps a single property yet compiles down to the underlying type at runtime—no extra object allocation. In **model.kt**, write:

```
@JvmInline
value class TaskId(val underlying: UUID)
```

We cannot pass a **TaskDescription** where a **TaskId** is expected. At runtime, **TaskId** is just a **UUID**. We then refactor our in-memory store from **Map<UUID, String>** to **Map<TaskId, TaskDescription>**. The compiler enforces correct usage and we gain self-documenting code.

Enhanced When Expressions

Stronger Exhaustiveness Checking

The Kotlin 2.0 flags missing **when** branches on sealed types more reliably. If we have:

```
sealed interface Command
object ListAll : Command
data class Add(val desc: String) : Command
```

```
object Remove : Command
```

and we write:

```
when(cmd) {
  is ListAll -> …
  is Add     -> …
}
```

the compiler warns us that **Remove** is unhandled.

Pattern-Based Matching

You can now use arbitrary conditions in **when** without requiring **else**. For example:

```
when {
  input.startsWith("add ") -> handleAdd(input.drop(4))
  input == "list"          -> handleList()
  input.matches(Regex("\\d+")) -> handleRemove(input.toInt())
}
```

This form reads as clean conditional logic, and the compiler enforces that all paths are considered if we opt in to exhaustive **when** via **-Xassertions**.

Refactoring Task Tracker Loop

Here, we replace our REPL's chain of **if-else** with:

```
when {
  input.startsWith("add ")        -> with(parser, service) {
handleAdd(input.drop(4)) }
  input == "list"                 -> with(service) {
handleList() }
  input.startsWith("remove ")     -> with(service) {
handleRemove(input.drop(7).toInt()) }
  input == "exit"                 -> return
  else                            -> println("Unknown command")
```

```
}
```

Your loop now reads like a table of commands, improving readability and maintainability.

Contracts and Improved Flow Analysis

What Are Contracts?

The Contracts let library authors inform the compiler about function behavior—such as null checks or invocation counts—so that flow analysis becomes smarter.

For example, the standard library's **require(value != null)** uses a contract to tell the compiler that after this check, **value** is non-null.

Custom Contract in Task Tracker

Suppose we write a helper:

```
import kotlin.contracts.*
fun requireNonEmpty(input: String) : String {
  contract { returns() implies (input.isNotEmpty()) }
  require(input.isNotEmpty()) { "Input cannot be empty" }
  return input
}
```

When we call **val desc = requireNonEmpty(raw)**, the compiler knows **desc** is non-empty thereafter. We avoid redundant null-or-empty checks later.

Sealed Interfaces and Hierarchies

Kotlin 2.0 allows **sealed interface Command** so we can implement commands across multiple files or modules, not just nested inside one class.

To apply, we define in **commands.kt**:

```
sealed interface Command
data class Add(val desc: String): Command
object ListAll : Command
data class Remove(val id: Int): Command
```

You can implement new commands in separate files—say, **UpdateCommand.kt**—and the compiler still enforces exhaustive **when** checks.

Standard-Library Extensions

The Kotlin 2.0 adds extensions like **List<T>.splitWhen { }** or **Map<K,V>.getOrThrow(key)** so we handle error cases idiomatically.

So for example, let us say that to partition tasks by status, we might have to write:

```
val (completed, pending) = tasksList.splitWhen { it.isDone }

println("Pending: ${pending.size}, Completed:
${completed.size}")
```

This single line replaces earlier verbose loop-and-filter code.

Summary

To sum it up, we looked at how Kotlin 2.0 had changed because of how it's been used in the industry, how well it works, and the language-level safety features it's got. When we installed OpenJDK `17, SDKMAN!, and the Kotlin `2.0.20 compiler on Linux, we also configured IntelliJ IDEA with Gradle Kotlin DSL, EditorConfig, Detekt, Ktlint, and other plugins. We confirmed that the Kotlinc and Gradle targeted version was 2.0.20, that the Task Tracker starter was imported, and that the basic REPL loop functioned.

You saw how Kotlin's 2.0 context-receivers got rid of parameter clutter, value classes delivered zero-overhead domain types, enhanced when expressions enforced exhaustiveness, and contracts improved flow analysis. We split up command parsing into different parts, used standard library extensions for collection operations, and saw how these features worked together to create short, clear code. Finally, we ran the refactored Task Tracker, and we verified that each modern syntax enhancement produced clearer, safer, and more maintainable code.

CHAPTER 2: VARIABLES, DATA TYPES, AND BASIC OPERATIONS

Chapter Overview

After chapter 1, we move on to this chapter wherein we explore how Kotlin distinguishes immutable and mutable variables—**val** versus **var**—and why that choice shapes program safety and clarity. We will declare the Task Tracker's in-memory store and ID counter, then experiment with primitive number types and **Char** values to handle identifiers, counters, and priority flags.

Next, we will explore arrays, lists, sets, and maps—practically applying each to store tasks, maintain insertion order, and enforce uniqueness. We will use **Pair** to return multiple values and destructure them for cleaner code. Afterward, we will dive into Boolean logic and operators to validate user input, combine conditions for filtering tasks, and implement commands that respond only when specific criteria are met.

And finally, we will become a string master—trimming, splitting with limits, case normalization, substring previews, string templates, and multi-line formatting. We will be able to sanitize input and generate polished console output. By the time we reach the end of this chapter, we will totally get how the data types and operations in Kotlin form the base for solid decision-making and data presentation in our TaskTracker application.

Variable Declarations and Mutability

We will now get into defining how our Task Tracker stores data in memory. At the core of any app, it needs a place to keep tasks—unique identifiers, descriptions, and status flags. Kotlin offers two fundamental ways to declare variables: **val** for immutable references and **var** for mutable ones. The choice between them shapes the safety and predictability of our code. So here, we will explore both, then apply them to establish the initial in-memory data structures that hold our tasks.

Understanding 'val' and 'var'

When we declare a variable with **val**, we create a read-only reference. Once assigned, it cannot point to a different object. Think of **val** as a constant handle: the data it refers to might be mutable internally, but the reference itself never changes. In contrast, **var** produces a mutable reference. We can reassign it at any time, pointing it to a new object or value.

```
val x: Int = 5          // x always refers to 5
var y: Int = 10         // y can be reassigned
y = 15                  // now y refers to 15
```

We can use **val** whenever possible to signal intent: "I do not plan to reassign this." This practice prevents accidental reassignments and helps the compiler optimize code. Reserve **var** for cases where we genuinely need to update the variable to refer to a new value or object.

Immutable vs. Mutable Collections

Kotlin's standard library distinguishes between immutable and mutable collection interfaces. An immutable **List<T>** does not allow adding or removing elements; a **MutableList<T>** does. We choose the interface according to how we intend to use the collection.

```
val readOnlyTasks: List<String> = listOf("A", "B")
val editableTasks: MutableList<String> = mutableListOf("A",
"B")
editableTasks.add("C")     // allowed
// readOnlyTasks.add("C") // compiler error
```

The exposure of immutable interfaces in APIs prevents external code from unexpectedly altering our data structures, thereby increasing robustness.

Establishing Task Store

At first, open the **Main.kt** in **src/main/kotlin/tracker/**. At the top of the **main** function, declare the in-memory store for tasks. We want to map task identifiers to descriptions. Later we will replace raw types with value classes; for now, use basic types to focus on **val** and **var**.

```
fun main() {
    // Immutable reference to a mutable map
    val tasks: MutableMap<Int, String> = mutableMapOf()
    var nextId: Int = 1
    // REPL loop begins here…
}
```

Here,

- **tasks** is declared with **val**, meaning the reference to the map never changes.
- The map itself is mutable, so we can add and remove entries.
- And, the **nextId** is a **var** because we will increment it each time we add a new task.

Mutability in Action

Inside the REPL loop, we handle **"add"** commands by inserting into the **tasks** map and then incrementing **nextId**.

```
while (true) {
    print("> ")
    val input = readLine().orEmpty()
    when {
        input.startsWith("add ") -> {
            val description = input.removePrefix("add ")
            tasks[nextId] = description        // mutating the
map
            println("Task added: $nextId")
            nextId++                           // mutating the
reference
        }
        input == "list" -> {
            tasks.forEach { (id, desc) ->
                println("$id: $desc")
            }
        }
        input == "exit" -> break
        else -> println("Unknown command")
    }
}
```

In the above:

- You read user input into an immutable **val input**.
- On **"add ..."**, we mutate the **tasks** map via **tasks[nextId] = description**.
- You mutate **nextId** itself by writing **nextId++**.

By minimizing **var** usage—only for **nextId**—you make the code's mutation points explicit.

Refactoring with Immutable Interfaces

Now to reinforce safe APIs, we need to expose **tasks** as an immutable **Map** when listing or passing to other components. Inside **main**, we still hold a **MutableMap**, but when we call a function to display tasks, require a **Map<Int, String>** parameter.

```
fun displayTasks(readOnlyTasks: Map<Int, String>) {
    if (readOnlyTasks.isEmpty()) println("No tasks found.")
    else readOnlyTasks.forEach { (id, desc) -> println("$id:
$desc") }
}
```

Then in our loop:

```
input == "list" -> displayTasks(tasks)
```

This pattern prevents accidental mutation within **displayTasks**. Even if that function grows more complex, the compiler enforces that it cannot change the task store.

Converting to Value Classes

Although we will dive deeper into value classes in Chapter 4, we can already start migrating primitive types to domain types. Replace **Int** with a **TaskId** value class and **String** with **TaskDescription**.

In a new file **model.kt**:

```
@JvmInline value class TaskId(val id: Int)
@JvmInline value class TaskDescription(val text: String)
```

Back in **Main.kt**, we then update the declarations:

```
val tasks: MutableMap<TaskId, TaskDescription> =
mutableMapOf()
var nextId = TaskId(1)
```

Here, the mutation remains the same:

```
tasks[nextId] = TaskDescription(description)
nextId = TaskId(nextId.id + 1)
```

The use of **val** for **tasks** and **var** for **nextId** confirms that only the identifier generator changes, while the task collection reference stays fixed.

Primitive and Complex Data Types

Number Types

Kotlin offers six primitive number types: **Byte**, **Short**, **Int**, **Long**, **Float**, and **Double**. Each type balances range and memory footprint. For task identifiers and simple counters, we typically use **Int**, which spans from -2^{31} to $2^{31}-1$. When we need to record timestamps in milliseconds or very large counters, **Long** becomes appropriate. If we later add estimated completion times with fractional minutes, **Double** handles decimal precision.

So here, we modify our **nextId** declaration within our **Main.kt** to demonstrate different number types:

```
var nextIntId: Int = 1                    // default counter

var nextLongId: Long = 1L                 // explicit Long
counter

val piApprox: Float = 3.14F               // sample Float value

val eApprox: Double = 2.718281828         // high-precision
Double
```

If we run the REPL and add tasks, we can print both counters side by side:

```
tasks[nextIntId] = description

println("Int ID: $nextIntId, Long ID: $nextLongId")

nextIntId++

nextLongId++
```

This shows how Kotlin enforces correct usage. It is appending **L** for **Long** and **F** for **Float**—while letting we mix types safely in expressions with automatic conversions where allowed.

Characters and String Interplay

A single character uses the **Char** type, enclosed in single quotes. Although we rarely store isolated characters in a Task Tracker, we might validate command prefixes or parse status flags. For example, we can check if the user's input begins with the character `'!'` to denote a high-priority task.

Just simply add the following snippet to our command parser:

```
val raw = readLine().orEmpty()
```

```
if (raw.firstOrNull() == '!') {
    val highPriority = true
    val commandText = raw.drop(1)
    println("High-priority command detected: $commandText")
}
```

In the above, the **firstOrNull()** returns a **Char?**, and comparing it to **'!'** leverages Kotlin's null-safe operators. We avoid a crash when the input is empty because **firstOrNull()** yields **null** rather than throwing an exception.

Arrays

An **Array<T>** holds a fixed number of elements of type **T**. We might use an array if we know in advance the maximum number of tasks we wish to support, or if we want to benchmark performance differences between arrays and lists.

In **Main.kt**, try inserting a temporary experiment as below:

```
val maxTasks = 100
val taskArray = arrayOfNulls<String>(maxTasks)  // initially
all null
```

When we add a task, place it into the next free slot:

```
if (nextIntId <= maxTasks) {
    taskArray[nextIntId - 1] = description
    println("Stored in array slot ${nextIntId - 1}")
} else println("Maximum tasks reached")
```

After you run this code, it will show that arrays require manual bounds checking. We will later prefer **MutableList** for dynamic sizing, but this exercise highlights how arrays work under the hood and why Kotlin distinguishes them from more flexible collections.

Lists, Sets, and Maps

A **List<T>** represents an ordered collection that we can traverse by index. Its mutable variant, **MutableList<T>**, lets us add and remove elements. In our Task Tracker, you've already used a **MutableMap** to pair IDs with descriptions. We can also maintain a separate **MutableList<TaskId>** to record insertion order or support undo operations.

Add after our map declaration:

```
val insertionOrder: MutableList<Int> = mutableListOf()
```

Inside the **"add"** branch:

```
tasks[nextIntId] = description
insertionOrder.add(nextIntId)
println("Task IDs in order: $insertionOrder")
```

After printing **insertionOrder**, we see how the list grows dynamically, unlike the fixed-size array.

Next, a **Set<T>** enforces uniqueness. If we want to track which task descriptions have appeared before, declare:

```
val uniqueDescriptions: MutableSet<String> = mutableSetOf()
```

Then in **"add"**:

```
if (uniqueDescriptions.add(description)) {
    println("New description recorded")
} else println("Duplicate description ignored")
```

This use-case prevents identical tasks from cluttering our tracker.

Pairs and Triples for Compound Values

Kotlin's **Pair<A,B>** and **Triple<A,B,C>** group two or three values without defining a custom class. We might use a **Pair** to return both a **TaskId** and its timestamp from a function.

For this, let us define a helper:

```
fun addTaskWithTimestamp(desc: String): Pair<Int, Long> {
    tasks[nextIntId] = desc
    val timestamp = System.currentTimeMillis()
    insertionOrder.add(nextIntId)
    return Pair(nextIntId, timestamp)
}
```

In our loop, we then call:

```
val (id, time) = addTaskWithTimestamp(description)
println("Task $id added at $time")
nextIntId++
```

The destructuring of declarations let us unpack the pair into **id** and **time** variables, keeping code concise.

All these types in our app are used to internalize how data is categorized by Kotlin and why each collection interface exists. The subsequent topic will elaborate on these foundations by introducing Boolean logic and operators, thereby empowering us to filter, query, and manipulate our task collections with precision.

Booleans and Logical Operators

Now that you have set up storage for tasks and experimented with numbers, characters, and collections, we will turn to decision logic. Boolean values (**true**/**false**) and logical operators (**&&**, **||**, **!**) lie at the heart of any interactive program. They let us test conditions, branch execution, and filter data.

Boolean Type and Comparison Operators

When we declare a Boolean in Kotlin, we write:

```
val flag: Boolean = true
var isActive: Boolean = false
```

The comparison operators yield Boolean results. Common forms include:

- **==** and **!=** for equality and inequality
- **<**, **>**, **<=**, **>=** for numeric comparisons

In **Main.kt**, we can add a quick check to ensure **nextIntId** never exceeds a threshold:

```
val maxTasks = 100
if (nextIntId > maxTasks) println("Cannot add more tasks")
```

In the above, the **nextIntId > maxTasks** evaluates to a Boolean. The **if** expression uses that value to decide whether to print the warning.

Logical Operators

We often come across a situation wherein we need to test multiple conditions at once. The Kotlin provides:

- *AND*: **&&** returns **true** only if both operands are **true**.
- *OR*: **||** returns **true** if at least one operand is **true**.
- *NOT*: **!** inverts a Boolean.

Let us take an example on Input Validation. Here, we ensure that an "add" command has non-empty description and does not exceed length limits:

```
val desc = input.removePrefix("add ").trim()
if (desc.isNotEmpty() && desc.length <= 50) {
    addTask(desc)
} else println("Description must be 1-50 characters")
```

The expression **desc.isNotEmpty() && desc.length <= 50** combines two Boolean tests. If either fails, the entire condition is **false**, and the task is rejected.

Null-Safe Boolean Expressions

When reading user input with **readLine()**, we get a **String?**. We must guard against **null** before calling methods on it. Kotlin's safe-call operator and the Elvis operator help:

```
val rawInput: String? = readLine()
val input = rawInput?.trim().orEmpty()  // converts null to ""
```

Now **input** is non-null, so we can apply Boolean checks without risking a null-pointer exception.

Boolean Logic in Task Filtering

Imagine adding a "filter" command to display only tasks whose descriptions contain a keyword and whose IDs fall within a range. Here, we parse two parameters: a keyword and a maximum ID.

We can extend our REPL loop to recognize:

```
input.startsWith("filter ")
```

We then extract arguments and convert the second to an integer safely:

```
val parts = input.removePrefix("filter ").split(" ")
```

```
val keyword = parts.getOrNull(0).orEmpty()
val maxId = parts.getOrNull(1)?.toIntOrNull() ?: Int.MAX_VALUE
```

Next, we then filter the tasks map:

```
val filtered = tasks.filter { (id, desc) ->
    desc.contains(keyword, ignoreCase = true) && id <= maxId
}
displayTasks(filtered)
```

In the above, the lambda's Boolean expression **`desc.contains(...) && id <= maxId`** uses both string-matching and numeric comparison to decide which entries to include.

Boolean Flags

Suppose we adopt a convention: prefixing a description with **`!`** marks it high priority. We can store a Boolean flag in a data class. For this, we define in **`model.kt`**:

```
data class Task(val id: TaskId, val description:
TaskDescription, val highPriority: Boolean = false)
```

We then modify our add logic:

```
val rawDesc = input.removePrefix("add ").trim()
val isHigh = rawDesc.firstOrNull() == '!'
val descText = if (isHigh) rawDesc.drop(1).trim() else rawDesc
val task = Task(nextId, TaskDescription(descText), isHigh)
service.createTask(task)
println("Task added: $nextId (high priority: $isHigh)")
```

Here, we used the Boolean expression **`rawDesc.firstOrNull() == '!'`** to set the flag. Later we can filter high-priority tasks with:

```
val highTasks = service.getAllTasks().filter { it.highPriority
}
displayTasks(highTasks.associate { it.id.id to
it.description.text })
```

Logical Operator Short-Circuiting

The Kotlin's **&&** and **||** operators are short-circuiting. In **A && B**, if **A** is **false**, **B** is not evaluated. This lets us chain null checks safely:

```
if (rawInput != null && rawInput.startsWith("add ")) { … }
```

If **rawInput** is **null**, the second check is skipped, avoiding an exception.

Composing Complex Conditions

You can group Boolean expressions with parentheses for clarity. For instance, only allow "remove" when ID is valid and the task is not high-priority:

```
val idToRemove = parts.getOrNull(0)?.toIntOrNull()
if (idToRemove != null && tasks.containsKey(idToRemove) &&
!service.isHighPriority(idToRemove)) {
    service.removeTask(idToRemove)
    println("Task $idToRemove removed")
} else println("Cannot remove task")
```

The combined condition uses **&&** and **!** to express: ID exists ***and*** task is not high priority. Grouping is implicit here, but we can add parentheses for readability.

We can carry all these skills into the next topic—string manipulation and formatting—where we refine how task descriptions appear to the user.

Manipulating Strings and Formatting Data

You begin by treating every user input as raw text that often includes extra spaces, inconsistent casing, or unexpected characters. In Kotlin, calling **trim()** on a **String** removes leading and trailing whitespace, so **"add task"** becomes **"add task"**.

Due to this, we write:

```
val rawInput = readLine().orEmpty()
val input = rawInput.trim()
```

When we normalize input at the start of our REPL loop, every subsequent parsing step can assume a clean **input**, preventing subtle bugs. If we only want to remove leading spaces, we call **trimStart()**, or **trimEnd()** for trailing only. These methods ensure commands like "

list" and "**list**" behave identically.

In Kotlin, the splitting of a **String** into meaningful parts uses **split** with a limit. We want to separate the command verb from its arguments only once. Here, we write:

```
val (command, args) = input.split(" ", limit = 2).let { it[0]
to it.getOrNull(1).orEmpty() }
```

With **limit = 2**, we guarantee that **args** retains spaces inside descriptions. When we type **add Buy milk and eggs**, we see **command == "add"** and **args == "Buy milk and eggs"**. Later, joining a list of tags back into a comma-separated string uses **joinToString(", ")**.

We can experiment with:

```
val tags = listOf("urgent", "home")

println("Tags: ${tags.joinToString()}")
```

Seeing "**Tags: urgent, home**" confirms that splitting and joining work seamlessly.

You then tackle case normalization so that filtering commands ignore letter case. By invoking **equals(other, ignoreCase = true)**, we match keywords regardless of how users type them. For example:

```
if (description.equals(filterKeyword, ignoreCase = true))
displayTasks(tasks)
```

You also capitalize the first character of display titles with **replaceFirstChar { it.uppercaseChar() }**, turning "**task tracker**" into "**Task tracker**". To preview long descriptions, we call **take(20)** and append an ellipsis when **length > 20**. We code:

```
val preview = description.take(20).let { if
(description.length > 20) "$it…" else it }

println("Preview: $preview")
```

This approach ensures that our command-line output never becomes overwhelming. Now in preparing reports, we can leverage Kotlin's multi-line strings as shown below:

```
val report = """

    |=== Task Report ===

    |ID: $id
```

```
    |Description: $preview
    |Priority: ${if (highPriority) "High" else "Normal"}
""".trimMargin()
println(report)
```

Here, the starting of each line with **|** and calling **trimMargin()**, the block aligns neatly. We then format timestamps using Java's **DateTimeFormatter** for human-readable time:

```
val timestamp = DateTimeFormatter.ofPattern("yyyy-MM-dd
HH:mm:ss")
    .withZone(ZoneId.systemDefault())
    .format(Instant.now())
println("Added at: $timestamp")
```

Seeing a clean, aligned report printed in our console reinforces how string manipulation and formatting combine to produce professional-grade CLI output.

Now we apply these techniques in a quick exercise for you, where you add a **search** command that finds tasks containing a keyword ignoring case, then prints results in an aligned two-column layout. Use **padStart()** to align IDs, **contains(..., ignoreCase = true)** for matching, and multi-line strings for headers. As we implement and run this feature, we witness firsthand how string operations transform raw input into structured, readable output—elevating our Task Tracker from a simple loop into a polished tool.

Summary

To review what we learned, we established in-memory storage for tasks using a **val** reference to a **MutableMap** and a **var** counter for IDs, making mutation points explicit. We distinguished between **val** and **var**, favoring immutable references wherever possible and limiting mutable references to clearly defined cases. We explored primitive number types—**Int**, **Long**, **Float**, **Double**—and used them to track task IDs, counters, and sample values.

Next, we handled single characters via **Char** to detect high-priority commands, and we experimented with fixed-size **Array** versus dynamic **MutableList** and **MutableSet**, observing how each collection type behaved when adding, iterating, and enforcing uniqueness. We grouped multiple return values with **Pair** to return both task ID and timestamp, then destructured the result for concise code. We applied Boolean logic and operators—**==**, **!=**, **<**, **>**, **&&**, **||**, **!**—to validate input, filter tasks by keyword and ID range, and guard against invalid or high-priority removals.

And finally, we manipulated strings with **`trim()`**, **`split(limit=2)`**, **`take()`**, and multi-line `"""..."""`**`.trimMargin()`** constructs to sanitize commands, extract arguments, preview long descriptions, and produce aligned, human-readable reports with embedded timestamps. Each of the technique reinforced how Kotlin's type system and standard-library functions collaborate to create safe, expressive, and maintainable code in our project.

Chapter 3: Control Structures and Program Flow

Chapter Overview

To begin with, we start to explore how Kotlin's **if-else** constructs enable precise decision-making in our Task Tracker, using both statement and expression forms to validate input, enforce limits, and generate unified messages. We will then adopt the more scalable **when** expression to map user commands and conditions to actions in a clear, maintainable dispatch table.

After that, we will implement **while** loops to drive the REPL loop and nested validation prompts, ensuring continuous responsiveness and robust input handling. We will see how background tasks—such as periodic reminders—use **while** with delays to avoid busy-waiting. Finally, we will employ **do-while** loops to guarantee that confirmation prompts and menus execute at least once before checking exit conditions, reducing code duplication and improving user experience. The whole chapter aims to transform our project's control flow into a concise, expressive set of constructs that handle every interaction reliably and readably.

If-Else Constructs

Decision logic is relied on in every layer of an application: when validating user input in forms, routing HTTP requests in web services, toggling feature flags in production, or selecting algorithms at runtime. The simplest building block for such decisions is the **if-else** construct. By evaluating a Boolean expression, **if-else** directs execution down one path or another, ensuring that only the intended code runs under specific conditions. In our Task Tracker, **if-else** governs whether to add a task, list existing tasks, remove a task, or exit the program. If we master both statement-style and expression-style **if-else**, it can guarantee that each branch remains clear, testable, and maintainable.

Statement vs. Expression Form

Statement Form

When side effects are performed directly in each branch, use **if-else** as a statement.

```
if (tasks.isEmpty()) {
    println("No tasks available.")
} else {
    println("You have ${tasks.size} tasks.")
}
```

This form executes one of the two **println** calls based on the condition but does not return a value.

Expression Form

If-else should be treated as an expression that yields a value. This approach separates decision logic from side effects.

```
val message = if (tasks.isEmpty()) {
    "No tasks available."
} else {
    "You have ${tasks.size} tasks."
}
println(message)
```

By computing **message** first, then printing once, we reduce duplication and clarify intent.

Refactoring "list"

First locate the branch handling **input == "list"**. Then replace the nested statement-style code with expression-style:

```
if (input == "list") {
    val output = if (tasks.isEmpty()) {
        "No tasks found."
    } else {
        tasks.entries.joinToString("\n") { (id, desc) -> "$id: $desc" }
    }
    println(output)
}
```

How this helps you?

- You compute display text in one place.
- You print once, avoiding repeated I/O calls.
- You make the decision logic easy to unit-test by extracting it later.

Chaining Conditions with 'Else-If'

When multiple exclusive checks are needed—such as enforcing a maximum task count and validating description length, it is good to chain **else if**:

```
if (tasks.size >= maxTasks) {
    println("Cannot add more tasks: limit reached.")
} else if (desc.isBlank() || desc.length > 50) {
    println("Description must be 1-50 characters.")
} else {
    tasks[nextId] = desc
    println("Task added: $nextId")
    nextId++
}
```

Following are the key benefits of it:

- Conditions evaluated top to bottom.
- Early branches prevent unnecessary checks.
- Mandatory braces maintain readability.

Nested Logic with Combined Booleans

The deep nesting can obscure intent, which is why it is important to be mindful of the connections between sentences. Put together Boolean tests into one condition and use expression form to handle results:

```
val valid = desc.isNotBlank() && desc.length <= 50 &&
!uniqueDescriptions.contains(desc)
val feedback = if (valid) {
    tasks[nextId] = desc
    uniqueDescriptions.add(desc)
    println("Task added: $nextId")
    nextId++
    "Success"
} else {
```

```
    when {
        desc.isBlank() -> "Description cannot be empty."
        desc.length > 50 -> "Description too long."
        else -> "Duplicate description."
    }
}
println(feedback)
```

Why we do this?

- You isolate validation logic in **`valid`**.
- You compute a single **`feedback`** message via **`if-else`** and nested **`when`**.
- You perform side-effects (adding, printing) inside the branch that succeeded, then print feedback only once.

Early Exit with 'Elvis'

Try using the Elvis operator (`?:`) for concise null checks in place of small **`if-else`** blocks. In our REPL loop:

```
val line = readLine()?.trim() ?: return  // exit on EOF or
null
```

This single line replaces:

```
val raw = readLine()
val line = if (raw != null) raw.trim() else return
```

By leveraging `?:`, we maintain explicit control flow while keeping code succinct.

"stats"

A "**`stats`**" command should be implemented to report counts of pending and high-priority tasks. The use of **`if-else`** is for the decision of the output message:

```
if (input == "stats") {
    val pending = tasks.count { !completedSet.contains(it.key)
}
    val high = highPrioritySet.size
```

```
    val message = if (pending == 0 && high == 0) {
        "No pending or high-priority tasks."
    } else {
        "Pending: $pending, High-priority: $high"
    }
    println(message)
}
```

By applying these patterns throughout our Task Tracker's REPL loop, we make every decision point explicit, testable, and maintainable. In the next topic, we will elevate our branching logic with **`when`** expressions—scalable, pattern-matching constructs that generalize **`if-else if`** chains.

'When' for Conditional Handling

You have seen how **`if-else`** chains route commands in the Task Tracker, but as conditions multiply, those chains grow verbose and harder to maintain. The Kotlin's **`when`** expression provides a clear, pattern-matching alternative that maps specific conditions to actions. Rather than evaluating multiple Boolean tests in sequence, we declare each case alongside its handling code. This structure reads like a dispatch table: each branch describes "when this occurs, do that."

Syntax and Expression Form

A **`when`** without an argument tests arbitrary Boolean expression:

```
when {
    input.startsWith("add ")       -> handleAdd(input.drop(4))
    input == "list"                -> handleList()
    input.startsWith("remove ")    ->
handleRemove(input.drop(7).toIntOrNull())
    input == "exit"                -> return
    else                           -> println("Unknown
command")
}
```

You write a series of conditions on the left, separated by new lines, and the arrow points to the action. Kotlin evaluates each condition top to bottom, executing the first matching branch. Because **when** is an expression, it can produce a value:

```
val result = when {
    tasks.isEmpty() -> "No tasks available"
    else            -> "You have ${tasks.size} tasks"
}
println(result)
```

This replaces nested **if-else** blocks with a single, unified construct.

Replacing 'If-Else' Chains

Art first, we need to go to **when**-style branch which we introduced earlier. And then confirm that each command maps to exactly one branch:

```
while (true) {
    print("> ")
    val input = readLine().orEmpty().trim()
    when {
        input.startsWith("add ")    -> with(parser, service) {
handleAdd(input.drop(4)) }
        input == "list"             -> with(service) {
handleList() }
        input.startsWith("remove ") -> with(service) {
handleRemove(input.drop(7).toIntOrNull()) }
        input == "stats"            -> with(service) {
handleStats() }
        input == "exit"             -> break
        else                        -> println("Unknown
command: \"$input\"")
    }
}
```

What we achieve?

- Single construct handles all commands.
- No nested braces for each branch.
- Readable mapping from condition to action.

'when' with Argument for Exact Matching

When we compare a single variable against constants, supply it as the argument:

```
when (command) {
    "add"    -> handleAdd(args)
    "list"   -> handleList()
    "remove" -> handleRemove(args.toIntOrNull())
    "stats"  -> handleStats()
    else     -> println("Unknown command: $command")
}
```

In the above, the **command** is a **String** derived by splitting **input**. Kotlin checks equality against each branch's constant. This form avoids repeating **input ==** on every line, focusing attention on the variable being dispatched.

'when' for Type and Range Checks

The Kotlin allows pattern matching beyond simple equality. We can test types, ranges, or collections of values:

```
when (val id = args.toIntOrNull()) {
    null                -> println("Invalid ID format")
    in 1..tasks.size    -> handleRemove(id)
    else                 -> println("ID out of range")
}
```

Here, the **null** branch handles parsing failures, **in 1..tasks.size** covers valid IDs, and. The **else** catches anything outside those ranges.

Sealed Class Commands and Exhaustive 'when'

When we model commands as a sealed interface, **when** ensures we handle every subtype. In **commands.kt**:

```
sealed interface Command
data class Add(val desc: String): Command
object ListAll: Command
data class Remove(val id: Int?): Command
object Stats: Command
object Exit: Command
```

The parsing yields a **Command** instance and then we dispatch:

```
fun execute(cmd: Command) = when (cmd) {
    is Add        -> handleAdd(cmd.desc)
    is ListAll    -> handleList()
    is Remove     -> handleRemove(cmd.id)
    is Stats      -> handleStats()
    is Exit       -> return
}
```

If we omit a branch, the compiler warns that **when** is not exhaustive. This guarantee prevents unhandled commands, boosting reliability.

Returning Values from 'when'

You can use **when** to compute values as well as control flow. For example, building user feedback after removal:

```
val message = when {
    id == null                       -> "Invalid ID."
    !tasks.containsKey(id)           -> "Task $id not found."
    highPrioritySet.contains(id)     -> "Cannot remove
high-priority task."
    else -> {
        tasks.remove(id)
        "Task $id removed."
    }
```

```
}
println(message)
```

This pattern centralizes all removal logic in one expression, making it easier to test and modify.

Combining Conditions in Single Branch

The multiple conditions can share the same action by separating with commas:

```
when (input) {
    "q", "quit", "exit" -> break
    else                -> println("Type \"exit\" to quit.")
}
```

We can group synonyms or aliases without repeating the action.

'when' without Else

When **when** operates on a sealed class or enum, we can omit **else** if we cover every case:

```
when (cmd) {
    is Add, is Remove, is ListAll, is Stats, is Exit ->
execute(cmd)
}
```

The compiler enforces exhaustiveness. The omission of **else** surfaces missing branches at compile time, rather than letting unexpected values slip through.

'While' Loops for Repetition

There are scenarios in which a block of code must repeat until a condition changes. The Kotlin's **while** loop checks its condition before each iteration, running the loop body only when that condition holds true. Think of it as a gatekeeper: before entering the loop, Kotlin asks, "Does this condition remain valid?" If the answer is **true**, the code inside executes; if **false**, the loop ends immediately. This pre-check behavior makes **while** ideal for tasks where we cannot predict the number of iterations in advance—reading user input until it meets criteria, polling a resource until data arrives, or iterating until an external flag flips. Because the condition is evaluated every time before looping, our application can remain responsive to changes in variables, user actions, or system state. We avoid infinite loops by ensuring the condition eventually becomes **false**, usually by mutating a variable inside the loop.

Implementing REPL Loop

Our Task Tracker uses a read–eval–print loop to interact with users continuously. So, we write:

```
while (true) {
    print("> ")
    val input = readLine().orEmpty().trim()
    when {
        input.startsWith("add ")     ->
handleAdd(input.drop(4))
        input == "list"              -> handleList()
        input.startsWith("remove ") ->
handleRemove(input.drop(7).toIntOrNull())
        input == "stats"             -> handleStats()
        input == "exit"              -> break
        else                         -> println("Unknown
command")
    }
}
```

This **while (true)** creates an endless loop that only stops when we call **break**. Each iteration prompts the user, reads and trims input, and dispatches commands via **when**. Because the loop immediately reevaluates after each command, our application stays ready for the next instruction. The users perceive a responsive interface: as soon as they press Enter, the loop processes the command and returns control to them without delay.

Validating Input with Nested 'While'

Before proceeding, you often need to ensure that certain commands include valid arguments. For instance, when removing a task, a numeric ID is required. Rather than handling invalid input with a one-off error, we can use a nested **while** loop to insist on correct input.

```
if (input.startsWith("remove ")) {
    var id: Int? = input.drop(7).toIntOrNull()
    while (id == null) {
        print("Please enter a valid numeric ID: ")
```

```
        id = readLine()?.toIntOrNull()
    }
    handleRemove(id)
}
```

In the above, the inner **while (id == null)** loop repeats the prompt until **id** becomes non-null. Each time the user types a non-numeric string, the loop runs again, preventing the removal logic from executing on invalid data. This pattern keeps our main REPL loop simple while encapsulating the validation in its own repetitive block.

Looping Over Task Collections

Beyond user input, we can apply **while** to internal processes. Suppose we want the Task Tracker to automatically remind users of overdue tasks every minute. We might spawn a background thread:

```
thread {
    while (true) {
        val now = System.currentTimeMillis()
        tasks.filter { it.value.dueTimestamp < now &&
!it.value.completed }
             .forEach { println("Reminder: Task ${it.key} is
overdue!") }
        Thread.sleep(60_000)  // wait one minute
    }
}
```

In this snippet, the **while (true)** loop runs indefinitely in a separate thread. Each cycle filters the **tasks** map for overdue, incomplete entries, prints reminders, then sleeps. The pre-condition check at the top of each iteration ensures that if we later introduce a flag to stop reminders—say, **var remindersEnabled = false**—you can change the loop header to **while (remindersEnabled)** and break out cleanly when needed.

Responsiveness and Busy-Waiting

A common pitfall with **while** loops is busy-waiting—continuously checking a condition without pause, which wastes CPU cycles. We avoid this by including delays (**Thread.sleep**) or by yielding control (**delay** in coroutines). In the REPL loop, we implicitly yield while waiting for

readLine(). In background loops, always include a sleep interval or integrate suspendable functions in coroutines:

```
GlobalScope.launch {
    while (remindersEnabled) {
        delay(60_000)
        checkOverdueTasks()
    }
}
```

By suspending rather than blocking, we keep threads free for other work.

'Do-While' Loops for Guaranteed Execution

The running of a block of code at least once is often necessary before checking whether to repeat it. In interactive applications, the display of a menu, prompt for confirmation, or performance of an initial setup step is desired regardless of state. A simple **while** loop tests its condition before running; therefore, if the condition is initially false, the loop never executes. In contrast, a **do-while** loop ensures that the body runs once unconditionally, and then repeats only if the condition remains true. This pattern stops code duplication and makes sure that setup or validation steps always occur at least one time.

'do-while' Syntax

The Kotlin's **do-while** syntax places the loop body before the condition check:

```
do {
    // code that runs at least once
} while (condition)
```

You can treat it as a post-condition loop. The body executes, then Kotlin evaluates **condition**. If **condition** is **true**, the body runs again; if **false**, execution continues after the loop. This ensures a guaranteed initial execution, followed by conditional repeats.

Implementing Confirmation Prompts

In our app, we may want to confirm destructive actions, such as removing all tasks. We prompt the user at least once, then repeat if they provide invalid input. So here, we replace a simple **if** confirmation with a **do-while** loop:

```
input == "clear" -> {
    var response: String
    do {
        print("Are we sure we want to delete all tasks? (y/n):
")
        response = readLine().orEmpty().trim().lowercase()
    } while (response != "y" && response != "n")
    if (response == "y") {
        tasks.clear()
        println("All tasks removed.")
    } else {
        println("Clear cancelled.")
    }
}
```

In the above, we declare **response** outside the loop. Here, the **do** block runs once, prompting the user, and the **while** condition checks if **response** is neither **"y"** nor **"n"**. If the user types anything else—empty string, typo—the loop repeats until we get a valid answer. By placing the prompt inside **do**, we avoid writing the prompt once before a **while** loop and again inside it.

At Least One Task Display

Imagine adding a "show menu" command that always displays choices once, then repeats until the user selects "back." So here, we implement:

```
input == "menu" -> {
    var choice: String
    do {
        println("""
            |Task Tracker Menu:
            |1. Add task
            |2. List tasks
            |3. Remove task
```

```
            |4. Back to REPL
        """.trimMargin())
        print("Enter choice (1-4): ")
        choice = readLine().orEmpty().trim()
        when (choice) {
            "1" -> handleAdd(promptDescription())
            "2" -> handleList()
            "3" -> handleRemove(promptForId())
        }
    } while (choice != "4")
}
```

As per the above, the Menu always appears at least once. The invalid choices (e.g. **"5"**, **"abc"**) trigger redisplay, and the Loop exits only when user selects **"4"**. Your REPL loop remains responsive: after exiting the menu loop, control returns to the main **while**, waiting for the next top-level command.

Combining 'do-while' with Context-Receivers

It is possible to incorporate context-receivers within the **do-while** body, thereby ensuring the maintenance of both our service and parser within the intended scope. For example:

```
input == "bulk-add" -> with(parser, service) {
    var entries: List<String>
    do {
        print("Enter tasks (comma-separated): ")
        entries = readLine().orEmpty().split(",").map {
it.trim() }.filter { it.isNotEmpty() }
    } while (entries.isEmpty())
    entries.forEach { handleAdd(it) }
}
```

In the above, we guarantee that at least one non-empty task description is entered. The loop repeats until **entries** contains at least one valid string.

Summary

To quickly summarize, we got strongly with the Kotlin's primary control structures. We used **`if-else`** both as statements and expressions to branch on user commands, validate input lengths, enforce task limits, and produce unified feedback messages. We learned to chain **`else if`** for multiple exclusive conditions, combine Boolean checks to flatten nested logic, and leverage the Elvis operator for concise null handling.

Next, we replaced lengthy **`if-else if`** sequences with **`when`** expressions, mapping command patterns to handler functions in a clear, table-like form. We saw how **`when`** with and without arguments supports constant matching, range tests, and sealed-class exhaustiveness, reducing boilerplate and catching unhandled cases at compile time. We explored **`while`** loops to keep our REPL responsive—prompting, reading, and dispatching commands continuously—and nested loops to validate removal IDs until users provided correct input. We even sketched a background reminders thread using **`while (true)`** with sleep intervals to illustrate polling without busy-waiting.

Finally, we introduced **`do-while`** loops for confirmation prompts and guaranteed menu displays, ensuring that critical code segments executed at least once before checking exit conditions.

Chapter 4: Functions and Modular Programming Techniques

Chapter Overview

This chapter is where we start putting together separate behaviors into reusable functions, turning raw code blocks into named units with well-defined inputs and outputs. We will define parameters and return types explicitly—using default and named arguments—to enforce type-safe interfaces in our TaskTracker. Next up, we will dive into higher-order functions and create custom wrappers for logging, retry logic, and event callbacks that can accept other functions as parameters. It's pretty cool to see how inline functions get rid of the lambda-allocation overhead while allowing mini-DSLs for batch processing.

Finally, we will get a handle on lambda expressions and collection pipelines—filter, map, sort, and forEach. That'll let us express data transformations in a concise, readable style. When we are done with the chapter, our TaskTracker code will have clear sections, reusable pieces, and clear functional constructs. This will get we ready for more advanced stuff like classes, constructors, and object-oriented design.

Creating Functions for Reusable Code

As logic grows, embedding everything in a single **`main`** function becomes unwieldy. The functions let us encapsulate discrete behaviors—parsing input, validating data, displaying results—into named units. Each function becomes a reusable building block, so when we need to change parsing rules or output formatting, we update one location rather than hunting through dozens of lines. This modular approach mirrors how libraries work: we call well-defined APIs instead of rewriting logic. Functions also improve readability by abstracting complex steps behind descriptive names. When we read **`handleAdd(description)`**, we instantly know what happens, without parsing implementation details. Furthermore, smaller functions simplify testing: we can verify that **`isValidDescription()`** works correctly in isolation before integrating it into the REPL loop.

Defining and Invoking Simple Functions

In Kotlin, we declare a function with the **`fun`** keyword, a name, optional parameters with types, and a return type. For example, extract the logic that displays tasks into its own function. In **`Main.kt`**, above **`main()`**, we write:

```
fun displayTasks(tasks: Map<Int, String>) {
    if (tasks.isEmpty()) {
        println("No tasks to display.")
    } else {
```

```
        tasks.entries.forEach { (id, desc) -> println("$id:
$desc") }
    }
}
```

We then replace the inline listing code inside the REPL loop with a call to **displayTasks(tasks)**. This single change moves four lines of logic into a named unit, instantly decluttering our loop.

When we run the program and type **list**, the behavior remains identical—but our **main** function now reads:

```
if (input == "list") displayTasks(tasks)
```

The readability soars because the intent ("display tasks") appears directly.

Extracting Input Parsing into Functions

The parsing of raw user input into a command and its arguments occurred inline previously. We need to factor that into a function returning a **Pair<String,String>**:

```
fun parseInput(input: String): Pair<String, String> {
    val parts = input.split(" ", limit = 2)
    val command = parts[0]
    val args = parts.getOrNull(1).orEmpty()
    return command to args
}
```

In our REPL loop, replace splitting logic with:

```
val (command, args) = parseInput(input)
when (command) {
    "add"    -> handleAdd(args)
    "list"   -> displayTasks(tasks)
    // …
}
```

By isolating parsing, we can refine splitting rules—such as supporting quoted arguments—inside

parseInput without touching the loop.

Returning Values and Expression-Body Functions

The functions can compute and return values. For simple one-liner logic, the Kotlin supports expression-body syntax:

```
fun isValidDescription(desc: String): Boolean =
    desc.isNotBlank() && desc.length <= 50 &&
!uniqueDescriptions.contains(desc)
```

Here, we replace the inline validation in **handleAdd** with a call to **isValidDescription(desc)**. The function name conveys intent, and its body concisely expresses the rule. We can now write:

```
if (isValidDescription(desc)) { addTask(desc) } else {
println("Invalid description.") }
```

This abstraction also aids testing: we write unit tests for **isValidDescription** covering edge cases without invoking our app's REPL.

Functions with Default and Named Parameters

Now here, when we create tasks, we often supply the description but rarely override priority or timestamp. We make use of default parameters so callers omit common values:

```
fun createTask(
    description: String,
    highPriority: Boolean = false,
    timestamp: Long = System.currentTimeMillis()
): Int {
    val id = nextId++
    tasks[id] = Task(description, highPriority, timestamp)
    return id
}
```

In our **"add"** handling, we simply call **createTask(desc)**. Later, if we detect a **!** prefix, we call **createTask(desc, highPriority = true)**. The named parameters clarify which argument we are overriding.

Modularizing Command Handlers

Now we move each command's logic into its own function. To do this, we define above **`main()`**:

```
fun handleAdd(args: String) {
    val desc = args.trim()
    if (isValidDescription(desc)) {
        val id = createTask(desc)
        println("Task added: $id")
    } else {
        println("Invalid description.")
    }
}
fun handleRemove(args: String) {
    val id = args.toIntOrNull()
    // removal logic…
}
```

Then our loop condenses to:

```
when (command) {
    "add"    -> handleAdd(args)
    "remove" -> handleRemove(args)
    // …
}
```

Here, each handler focuses solely on its concern. We can later move these functions into a separate file—**`Commands.kt`**—organizing code by feature.

Higher-Order Functions

The Kotlin treats functions as first-class citizens. We can write functions that accept other functions. For example, we can log every command execution:

```
fun withLogging(commandName: String, action: () -> Unit) {
```

```
    println("Executing $commandName...")
    action()
    println("$commandName completed.")
}
```

We then wrap handler calls:

```
when (command) {
    "add"    -> withLogging("add") { handleAdd(args) }
    "list"   -> withLogging("list") { displayTasks(tasks) }
    // …
}
```

This higher-order function prints pre- and post-messages around any action, without modifying each handler. We have implemented a cross-cutting concern (logging) in a reusable way.

Defining Parameters and Return Types

Although we know that functions encapsulate behavior, their power comes from well-defined inputs and outputs. The parameters allow us to pass data into a function, and return types indicate what the function yields. Specifying parameter and return types explicitly creates clear contracts: "give me a **String**; I will return an **Int**." The compiler enforces those contracts, preventing inadvertent type mismatches and making our code more predictable. In the Task Tracker, functions such as **createTask(description: String): Int** accept a description and return the new task's identifier. Consumers of that function know exactly what to supply and what to expect.

Declaring Parameters

The Kotlin syntax for parameters places them in parentheses after the function name, each with a name and type:

```
fun handleAdd(description: String, highPriority: Boolean) { …
}
```

Here, the **description: String** ensures only text flows in, and the **highPriority: Boolean** signals a two-state flag.

Parameters are **val** by default—you cannot reassign them within the function—guaranteeing the input remains stable.

Let us take an example of parsing the input. Here, we refactor our inline parsing into a function with two parameters: the raw input and the delimiter:

```
fun splitCommand(input: String, delimiter: String = " "):
Pair<String,String> {
    val parts = input.split(delimiter, limit = 2)
    val cmd = parts[0]
    val args = parts.getOrNull(1).orEmpty()
    return cmd to args
}
```

In this, we used a default parameter **`delimiter: String = " "`**, so callers can omit it. The function signature documents exactly what inputs it handles.

Next, in our REPL loop, we now write:

```
val (command, args) = splitCommand(input)
```

This call works whether we supply one or two arguments.

Optional and Named Parameters

When functions have multiple parameters, the Kotlin's named-argument syntax enhances readability:

```
fun createTask(
    description: String,
    highPriority: Boolean = false,
    timestamp: Long = System.currentTimeMillis()
): Int { … }
```

The calling code can override only the parameter we care about:

```
createTask(description = desc, highPriority = true)
```

This clarity prevents mixing up Boolean flags or forgetting the meaning of positional arguments.

Specifying Return Types

Kotlin requires us declare a function's return type when it is not **Unit** (void). The syntax follows the parameter list:

```
fun calculateStats(tasks: Map<Int, Task>): Pair<Int,Int> { … }
```

In the above, the **Pair<Int,Int>** indicates two integers returned, for example pending and high-priority counts.

For example, think of computing the statistics, wherein we move our inline stats logic into:

```
fun computeStats(tasks: Map<Int, Task>): Pair<Int,Int> {
    val pending = tasks.count { !it.value.completed }
    val high    = tasks.count { it.value.highPriority }
    return pending to high
}
```

In the REPL loop:

```
val (pendingCount, highCount) = computeStats(tasks)
```

The compiler enforces that we destructure exactly two values of type **Int**. If we attempt to assign to three variables, we get a compile-time error.

Expression-Body Functions

Now when a function body is a single expression, we can combine its definition and return type succinctly:

```
fun isValidId(id: Int?, tasks: Map<Int, Task>): Boolean =
    id != null && tasks.containsKey(id)
```

This form makes the parameter and return contract prominent and reduces boilerplate.

Unit Return and Side-Effect Functions

The functions that perform actions without returning a value use the **Unit** return type, which we may omit:

```
fun displayMenu(): Unit { … }
fun displayMenu() { … }   // same effect
```

the above ones can be used for printing, logging, or modifying shared state. By contrast, functions that compute data always declare non-Unit returns.

Type Safety in Handlers

This is done by defining our command handlers with precise signatures to prevent misuse:

```
fun handleRemove(id: Int?, tasks: MutableMap<Int, Task>):
Boolean {
    if (id == null || !tasks.containsKey(id)) return false
    tasks.remove(id)
    return true
}
```

The return **Boolean** indicates success or failure. Also, the caller can react:

```
val removed = handleRemove(parsedId, tasks)
println(if (removed) "Removed." else "Failed to remove.")
```

The separation of concerns and explicit types shield our REPL loop from low-level details.

Higher-Order Functions with Typed Parameters

We also know that Kotlin allows parameters that are functions themselves. For example, we might abstract retry logic:

```
fun <T> retry(
    times: Int,
    block: () -> T
): T? {
    repeat(times - 1) {
        try { return block() } catch (_: Exception) {}
    }
    return try { block() } catch (_: Exception) { null }
}
```

Here, the **block: () -> T** declares a parameter of function type. The return type **T?** captures possible failure.

Apart from this, we can use the following when saving tasks:

```
val result = retry(3) { saveTasksToDisk(tasks) }
println(if (result != null) "Saved." else "Save failed.")
```

The functions become self-documenting contracts, compile-time checks catch mismatches, and our code gains modularity and clarity—preparing we for advanced topics such as higher-order functions and coroutines.

Implementing Higher-Order Functions

As you have seen previously, named functions encapsulate discrete behaviors in the Task Tracker, such as parsing input, validating descriptions, and handling commands. Higher-order functions build on this modularity by enabling us to pass functions as parameters or return them as results. This capacity transforms functions into top-tier elements: we can construct reusable frameworks that incorporate custom logic, implement the same control flow for different operations, and consolidate overarching concerns without replicating code. For example, instead of writing logging calls before and after every handler, we create a single higher-order function that wraps any action with logging. So, when our application is growing and we're adding features like bulk updates, network saves, or transaction management, higher-order functions let us inject behavior dynamically. This keeps the core logic clean and focused.

Function Types and Syntax

In Kotlin, a function type is written as **`(A, B) -> R`**, where **`A`** and **`B`** are parameter types and **`R`** is the return type. For example, a simple predicate on task descriptions uses the type **`(String) -> Boolean`**. In the following, we declare a parameter of that type inside another function:

```
fun filterTasks(
    tasks: Map<Int, String>,
    predicate: (String) -> Boolean
): Map<Int, String> {
    return tasks.filterValues { predicate(it) }
}
```

Here, the **`predicate`** is a parameter that accepts any function matching **`(String) -> Boolean`**. Within **`filterTasks`**, we call **`predicate(it)`** to decide which tasks to keep.

This abstraction decouples filtering logic from the storage structure, enabling we to reuse **filterTasks** with different criteria.

Retry Mechanism with Higher-Order Functions

Just imagine saving tasks to a disk or remote server where failures occasionally occur. We can write a generic retry function that accepts any suspending or regular block.

```
fun <T> retry(
    times: Int = 3,
    block: () -> T
): T? {
    var currentAttempt = 0
    while (currentAttempt < times) {
        try {
            return block()
        } catch (e: Exception) {
            currentAttempt++
            println("Attempt $currentAttempt failed:
${e.message}")
        }
    }
    return null
}
```

We can use the following when exporting tasks to JSON:

```
val success = retry(3) { saveTasksToJson(tasks) }
println(if (success != null) "Export succeeded" else "Export
failed after retries")
```

This pattern pushes retry logic into one place and lets us apply it to any operation that might throw, from database writes to network calls.

Event Hooks and Callbacks

We might allow clients of our Task Tracker to register hooks that run when tasks change. To do this, we simply define as below:

```
typealias TaskListener = (taskId: Int, description: String) ->
Unit
val onTaskAddedListeners = mutableListOf<TaskListener>()
fun addTaskListener(listener: TaskListener) {
    onTaskAddedListeners.add(listener)
}
fun notifyTaskAdded(id: Int, desc: String) {
    onTaskAddedListeners.forEach { it(id, desc) }
}
```

In **createTask**, invoke **notifyTaskAdded(id, description)**. Elsewhere, we register behavior:

```
addTaskListener { id, desc ->
    println("Listener: new task $id -> $desc")
}
```

This callback style—functions passed into registration methods—enables extensibility without changing core logic.

Combining Higher-Order Functions with Lambdas

The Kotlin's concise lambda syntax makes higher-order functions effortless. When calling **filterTasks**, we pass a lambda directly:

```
val urgentTasks = filterTasks(tasks) { desc ->
desc.startsWith("!") }
displayTasks(urgentTasks)
```

Or even more succinct:

```
filterTasks(tasks) { it.length > 20 }
```

After this, we can see how inline lambdas, combined with a generic filtering function, let us express complex queries in a single line while reusing the same **filterTasks** implementation.

Lambda Expressions for Concise Code

The encapsulation of parsing, validation, and command handling in our app is achieved through the use of named functions. However, many modern programming frameworks and libraries rely heavily on small, anonymous functions—known as lambdas—to express logic inline without ceremony. Lambda expressions changed the way developers write event handlers, callbacks, and collection transformations. In UI toolkits, for example, we attach a lambda to a button click rather than defining a separate listener class. In reactive streams, we pass lambdas to filter, map, and reduce data flows. Lambdas let us add behavior exactly where we need it. This makes our code easier to read. When reading code that uses lambdas, the transformation logic is visible right where the data is processed, eliminating the need to jump across multiple function definitions.

Lambda Syntax and Inline Function

In Kotlin, we write a lambda by placing parameters, the arrow token **`->`**, and the body inside curly braces. For example, a function type **`(Int) -> Boolean`** can be represented by a lambda:

```
val isEven: (Int) -> Boolean = { number -> number % 2 == 0 }
```

You can omit parameter types when they can be inferred:

```
val isOdd: (Int) -> Boolean = { it % 2 != 0 }
```

In the above, the **`it`** refers to the single implicit parameter. Functions that accept lambdas as parameters are called higher-order functions. We have already used **`filterTasks(tasks) { desc -> desc.startsWith("!") }`**. Kotlin also lets us mark a function **`inline`**, instructing the compiler to substitute the lambda's bytecode directly at the call site, avoiding the overhead of object creation for each lambda.

For example:

```
inline fun <T> measure(actionName: String, block: () -> T): T
{ … }
```

By inlining, we maintain the abstraction without runtime cost.

Applying Lambdas to Collections

You maintain a **`MutableMap<Int, Task>`** in memory. To list only high-priority tasks, we once wrote:

```
val highPriority = tasks.filter { entry ->
entry.value.highPriority }
```

```
highPriority.forEach { (id, task) -> println("$id:
${task.description}") }
```

With lambdas and method chaining, this becomes a one-liner:

```
tasks.filterValues { it.highPriority }
      .forEach { (id, t) -> println("$id: ${t.description}") }
```

You see the lambda **`{ it.highPriority }`** right at the filtering step, and the print logic inline in **`forEach`**. No need for temporary lists or separate loops. When we implement a search by keyword, we write:

```
tasks.filterValues { it.description.contains(keyword,
ignoreCase = true) }
      .forEach { (id, t) -> println("$id: ${t.description}") }
```

This pattern applies to sorting, mapping to CSV lines, or grouping by due date:

```
tasks.entries
      .sortedBy { it.value.dueTimestamp }
      .map { (id, t) ->
"$id,${t.description},${t.dueTimestamp}" }
      .forEach(::println)
```

Each transformation step uses a lambda, making the pipeline explicit and readable.

Custom Inline Functions and DSL-Like

Our own inline functions can be defined that accept lambdas so repetitive patterns can be factored out. For example, you could log the execution time of any code block.

```
inline fun <T> timed(label: String, block: () -> T): T {
    val start = System.nanoTime()
    val result = block()
    val duration = (System.nanoTime() - start) / 1_000_000
    println("$label took ${duration}ms")
    return result
}
```

We can use it when loading or saving tasks:

```
timed("Saving tasks") { saveTasksToDisk(tasks) }
```

Because we marked **timed** as **inline**, there's no lambda-object allocation at runtime. We can also create a mini-DSL for batch operations on tasks:

```
fun tasksBatch(process: MutableMap<Int, Task>.() -> Unit) {
    tasks.process()
}
```

Then call:

```
tasksBatch {
    filterValues { !it.completed }.forEach { (id, _) ->
remove(id) }
    println("Cleared pending tasks")
}
```

Now here, inside the lambda, **this** refers to our **tasks** map. The code reads like a domain-specific language: "in a batch, remove pending tasks and then print."

So, if we adopt lambda expressions and inline functions, we'll be able to cut down on all that boilerplate code, keep the business logic right where it's needed, and build flexible, composable pipelines in our TaskTracker. Our code will resemble a clear description of transformations more than plumbing, unlocking the full power of Kotlin's functional features.

Summary

So, to sum things up, we took the repeated logic and put it into some well-named functions, and we took our app and split it into some smaller parts. We defined functions with clear parameters and return types—using default and named arguments—to create tasks, parse input, and compute statistics with type-safe contracts. You've used higher-order functions that accept lambdas, like logging wrappers, retry mechanisms, and custom filtering, which makes it possible to have cross-cutting concerns and generic pipelines without duplicating code.

Next, we then used lambda expressions and inline functions to process collections in a concise way—filtering, mapping, sorting, and batching tasks through chained calls. Then we built mini-DSLs for batch operations and measured execution time with inline lambdas, reducing boilerplate and focusing on business logic. With destructuring, expression-body functions, and function types, you've got a codebase where each module does one thing well, handlers read like direct instructions, and shared behaviors live in reusable abstractions.

CHAPTER 5: OBJECT-ORIENTED CONSTRUCTS AND CLASS DESIGN

Chapter Overview

We begin this chapter by defining a **Task** class with a primary constructor to group related properties—ID, description, priority, completion flag, and timestamp—into a cohesive entity. We will try to add secondary constructors and **init** blocks to support alternate initialization scenarios and enforce invariants at creation time. Next, we will introduce a **CommandHandler** interface and implement concrete handlers for each command, then use polymorphic dispatch to decouple our main loop from specific command logic.

After that, we will factor shared behavior into an abstract base class, using **protected** methods to share logging and error handling only with subclasses. We will then apply Kotlin's visibility modifiers—**private**, **internal**, and **public**—to hide implementation details in **TaskService** and expose only stable, read-only APIs. Overall, we can have our app well structured with object-oriented principles that ensure code reuse, clear separation of concerns, and robust data security for future extension.

Defining Classes and Initializing Properties

We have so far managed tasks as raw maps of integers to strings, but the changed needs like tracking priority flags, timestamps, completion status, or tags, we will need a structured way to group related data and behavior. The Object-oriented programming gives us that structure by letting we define classes: blueprints for entities that bundle properties and functions together. In Kotlin, the classes provide a clear contract for what each object contains and how it behaves. If we try to model our Task Tracker's tasks as instances of a **Task** class rather than loose map entries, we gain stronger type safety, self-documenting code, and the ability to attach methods directly to the data they operate on. We no longer pass around unstructured parameters; instead, we work with well-defined objects whose constructors ensure that every instance begins life in a valid state.

Declaring Kotlin Class with Primary Constructor

So here, we can try to declare a class and its primary constructor in a single line. For this, we create **src/main/kotlin/tracker/Task.kt** and define the following:

```
package tracker
data class Task(
    val id: Int,
    val description: String,
    val highPriority: Boolean = false,
```

```
    var completed: Boolean = false,
    val createdTimestamp: Long = System.currentTimeMillis()
)
```

Now, in the above:

- The **data** modifier signals that this class is primarily for holding data. Kotlin automatically generates **equals()**, **hashCode()**, **toString()**, and **copy()** methods.
- **val id: Int** and **val description: String** define read-only properties initialized by the constructor. Once set, they cannot change, ensuring the identity and core text of a task remain stable.
- **val highPriority: Boolean = false** uses a default value so that callers need only specify priority when it differs from normal.
- **var completed: Boolean = false** declares a mutable property we will toggle when users mark tasks done.
- **val createdTimestamp: Long = System.currentTimeMillis()** captures the creation moment automatically, without extra code in **main**.

After grouping all five properties in the primary constructor, we have a concise, self-documenting definition of what constitutes a **Task**.

'init' Block for Validation

Sometimes we need to enforce additional invariants or compute derived properties when an object is created. The Kotlin's **init** block runs immediately after the primary constructor.

For example, to ensure descriptions are non-empty, we extend **Task.kt** as below:

```
init {
    require(description.isNotBlank()) { "Task description
cannot be blank." }
}
```

If someone attempts to create **Task(id = 1, description = "")**, the constructor throws an **IllegalArgumentException** with our message. This early validation moves error checking into the class itself, so other code can assume any **Task** instance is valid.

Instantiating and Managing Task Objects

Within the **Main.kt**, we replace our existing map of **MutableMap<Int, String>** with **MutableMap<Int, Task>**. At the top of **main()**, we then declare the following:

```
val tasks: MutableMap<Int, Task> = mutableMapOf()
var nextId = 1
```

Next, we update our "**add**" handler to create a **Task** object instead of a raw string:

```
val task = Task(
    id = nextId,
    description = desc,
    highPriority = desc.startsWith("!"),
)
tasks[nextId] = task
println("Task added: $task")
nextId++
```

Now here, when we print the **task**, Kotlin's generated **toString()** yields something like **Task(id=1, description=Buy milk, highPriority=false, completed=false, createdTimestamp=162243...)**, giving we rich insight without manual formatting.

Accessing and Modifying Properties

Later, when the users mark a task complete, we retrieve the object and update its mutable property:

```
val task = tasks[id]
if (task != null) {
    task.completed = true
    println("Marked complete: $task")
}
```

Because **completed** is a **var**, we can toggle it in place. We preserve the same object identity in the map, and other code that holds a reference to this **Task** sees the updated state immediately. By means of this topic, we converted two-dimensional data structures into complex objects, establishing the basis for inheritance, interfaces, and encapsulation in the upcoming subjects.

Primary and Secondary Constructors

We have already used the primary constructor in Kotlin's concise **data class Task(...)** declaration to bundle properties into objects. The primary constructor defines the core way to instantiate every object, setting up all essential properties at once. Secondary constructors—declared with **constructor(...)** inside the class—give we alternate ways to create instances, perhaps supplying default values, performing extra setup, or supporting legacy code patterns. While primary constructors shine for straightforward initialization, secondary constructors let us encapsulate more complex creation logic without cluttering the main signature.

Defining Secondary Constructor

To do this, inside our **Task.kt**, after the primary constructor and any **init** blocks, we add a secondary constructor to support creating a high-priority task from only an ID and description string prefixed with **!**.

Following is the syntax:

```
data class Task(
    val id: Int,
    val description: String,
    val highPriority: Boolean = false,
    var completed: Boolean = false,
    val createdTimestamp: Long = System.currentTimeMillis()
) {
    // Secondary constructor delegates to primary
    constructor(id: Int, rawDescription: String) : this(
        id = id,
        description = rawDescription.trimStart('!'),
        highPriority = rawDescription.startsWith("!")
    )
}
```

In the above:

- The secondary constructor takes **(id, rawDescription)**.
- It delegates to the primary constructor via **: this(...)**, computing **description** and **highPriority** based on the raw string.
- You keep all property initialization centralized in the primary constructor and **init** block, while the secondary constructor focuses on parsing logic.

Using Both Constructors

In **Main.kt**, when handling **"add"** commands, we previously wrote:

```
val desc = args.trim()
val task = Task(id = nextId, description = desc, highPriority
= desc.startsWith("!"))
```

Here, we replace that with a call to the secondary constructor, handing it the raw argument (with or without **!**):

```
val task = Task(nextId, args)    // uses secondary constructor
tasks[nextId] = task
println("Task added: $task")
nextId++
```

Now, whether **args** begins with **!** or not, the secondary constructor parses and delegates correctly. Our REPL loop remains clean—just one constructor call—while all parsing logic lives inside **Task.kt**.

Chaining Multiple Secondary Constructors

We can also define additional secondary constructors for other common patterns. For instance, if we often create tasks with a preset due date, add:

```
constructor(id: Int, description: String, dueInHours: Long) :
this(
    id = id,
    description = description,
    highPriority = false,
    completed = false,
    createdTimestamp = System.currentTimeMillis() + dueInHours
* 3_600_000
)
```

We then call it with:

```
val timedTask = Task(nextId, "Submit report", dueInHours = 24)
```

```
tasks[nextId] = timedTask
```

By overloading constructors, we support multiple creation scenarios without duplicating initialization code.

Through primary and secondary constructors, we now support flexible, type-safe creation of **Task** objects in multiple scenarios, keeping our class design robust and our application code concise.

Implementing Inheritance and Interfaces

The way in which functions and data classes organize our TaskTracker's logic has been seen, yet as features are multiplied—such as different storage backends, multiple command types, or notification behaviors—the risk of similar code being duplicated across modules is increased. The solution to this problem is provided by inheritance and interfaces, which enable the definition of common behavior once and its sharing across multiple types. When we inherit from a base class, we reuse its properties and methods without rewriting them. When we implement an interface, we commit to a set of required methods while retaining flexibility in each implementation. Together, these object-oriented mechanisms reduce boilerplate code, centralize maintenance, and enable us to extend functionality with minimal friction. We can add a new command type or storage strategy simply by subclassing or implementing an interface, knowing that the shared behavior is centralized. This helps us make our code better and faster.

Defining CommandHandler Interface

In our REPL loop, each command—add, list, remove, stats—was handled by a separate function. To unify this, define an interface **CommandHandler** that declares a single method for executing a command:

```
package tracker.commands
interface CommandHandler {
    val commandName: String
    fun execute(args: String)
}
```

Here, the **commandName** identifies which input this handler responds to. And, the **execute** runs the action with given arguments. By coding against this interface, our main loop need only look up handlers in a map and invoke **execute**, without knowing details of each command.

Implementing Handlers via Inheritance

To do this, we create concrete classes that implement **CommandHandler**. For "add" and "remove," we write:

```
class AddHandler(
    private val service: TaskService
) : CommandHandler {
    override val commandName = "add"
    override fun execute(args: String) {
        val task = Task(service.nextId(), args.trim())
        service.addTask(task)
        println("Added: $task")
    }
}
class RemoveHandler(
    private val service: TaskService
) : CommandHandler {
    override val commandName = "remove"
    override fun execute(args: String) {
        val id = args.toIntOrNull()
        if (service.removeTask(id)) println("Removed $id")
        else println("Cannot remove $id")
    }
}
```

Here, both classes share no duplicated logic: parsing **args**, printing results, and delegating to **service**. Yet they each implement the same interface.

Dispatching via Polymorphism

In **Main.kt**, we then register handlers in a list and dispatch dynamically:

```
val service = TaskService()
val handlers: List<CommandHandler> = listOf(
```

```
    AddHandler(service),
    RemoveHandler(service),
    ListHandler(service),
    StatsHandler(service)
)
while (true) {
    print("> ")
    val input = readLine().orEmpty().trim()
    val (cmd, args) = parseInput(input)
    handlers.find { it.commandName == cmd }?.execute(args)
        ?: println("Unknown command: $cmd")
}
```

By this, we no longer maintain a **when** or **if-else** chain. Adding a new handler means creating a class implementing **CommandHandler** and adding it to **handlers**. The dispatch logic remains untouched.

Abstract Base Classes for Shared Logic

Sometimes handlers share more than just an interface—perhaps they all need logging or error handling. To do this, we define an abstract base class that implements **CommandHandler** and provides common behavior:

```
abstract class BaseHandler(
    override val commandName: String,
    private val service: TaskService
) : CommandHandler {
    override fun execute(args: String) {
        try {
            println("Executing $commandName")
            handle(args)
        } catch (e: Exception) {
            println("Error in $commandName: ${e.message}")
```

```
        }
    }
    protected abstract fun handle(args: String)
}
```

Then refactor **AddHandler** to inherit from **BaseHandler**:

```
class AddHandler(service: TaskService) : BaseHandler("add",
service) {
    override fun handle(args: String) {
        val task = Task(nextId(), args.trim())
        service.addTask(task)
        println("Added: $task")
    }
}
```

Here, we moved logging and exception-catching into **BaseHandler**. All subclasses inherit that behavior automatically, eliminating repeated try/catch blocks.

Modeling Storage with Interfaces

Beyond commands, we may support different storage backends—memory, JSON file, or database. To do this, we define an interface **TaskRepository**:

```
interface TaskRepository {
    fun save(tasks: Map<Int, Task>)
    fun load(): Map<Int, Task>
}
```

Then implement two versions:

```
class InMemoryRepository : TaskRepository {
    private var store = mutableMapOf<Int, Task>()
    override fun save(tasks: Map<Int, Task>) { store =
tasks.toMutableMap() }
    override fun load() = store.toMap()
```

```
}
class JsonFileRepository(private val path: String) :
TaskRepository {
    override fun save(tasks: Map<Int, Task>) {
        File(path).writeText(serializeToJson(tasks))
    }
    override fun load(): Map<Int, Task> =
        deserializeFromJson(File(path).readText())
}
```

Our **TaskService** depends on **TaskRepository**, not a concrete class:

```
class TaskService(private val repo: TaskRepository) {
    private val tasks = repo.load().toMutableMap()
    fun addTask(task: Task) { tasks[task.id] = task;
repo.save(tasks) }
    // …
}
```

Switching storage does not require changing the service or handlers. The only necessary change is to inject a different repository implementation.

This establishes clear extension points for commands and storage. The reuse of shared logic via base classes and adherence to contracts via interfaces by our app modules ensures that the addition of new features involves minimal code changes and maximal reuse.

Enforcing Encapsulation and Data Security

So, as our app went from just maps and basic functions to more complex services, handlers, and repositories, we started to run into problems. It was like, if we didn't keep a close eye on access to our internal data structures, it could lead to inconsistencies and hidden bugs. The mutable state and helper logic are confined behind controlled interfaces by encapsulation, ensuring that every change to tasks is validated, persisted, and logged. By using Kotlin's visibility modifiers—**private**, **protected**, **internal**, and **public**—you draw clear boundaries between what parts of our code are implementation details versus public API. This separation prevents accidental misuse, simplifies reasoning about invariants, and makes future refactoring safe: we know exactly which methods and properties outside a class may call.

Applying 'private' to Guard Internal State

In **TaskService.kt**, we previously declared

```
class TaskService(private val repo: TaskRepository) {
    val tasks = repo.load().toMutableMap()
    // …
}
```

We then change **tasks** to **private**:

```
private val tasks = repo.load().toMutableMap()
```

Now no code outside **TaskService** can read or modify the map directly. All access must go through the service's public methods—**addTask**, **removeTask**, **getAllTasks**—which enforce validation and save changes.

Likewise, helper methods that should remain internal implementation details belong behind private visibility. If we have

```
fun validateDescription(desc: String) = desc.isNotBlank() &&
desc.length <= 50
```

we then make it private:

```
private fun validateDescription(desc: String) = …
```

This ensures that only **TaskService** methods invoke validation—command handlers cannot bypass the rule.

Exposing Read-Only Views with Map Copies

Now here, to let callers inspect tasks without granting mutation rights, we simply change:

```
fun getAllTasks(): Map<Int, Task> = tasks.toMap()
```

By returning a fresh **Map** copy, we prevent clients from casting back to **MutableMap** and altering our internal store. Attempting **service.getAllTasks() as MutableMap** now fails at runtime or compile time.

Using 'protected' for Subclass-Only Methods

In **BaseHandler**, we factored common logging into methods. Mark these **protected** so only subclasses see them:

```
abstract class BaseHandler(...) : CommandHandler {
    protected fun logStart() { … }
    protected fun logEnd()   { … }
    override fun execute(args: String) {
        logStart(); handle(args); logEnd()
    }
    protected abstract fun handle(args: String)
}
```

If we try calling **logStart()** from outside the class hierarchy, the compiler rejects it. This enforces that logging remains an inherited concern, not a general utility.

Leveraging internal for Module-Level Hiding

If we split code into modules—say, **core** and **cli**—mark classes in **core** not meant for public consumption as **internal**. In **core/src/main/kotlin**:

```
internal class AuditLogger { … }
internal fun recordAudit(entry: String) { … }
```

The **cli** module cannot see these symbols, reducing API surface and preventing misuse.

With all this, we guaranteed that every interaction with our Task Tracker's core state passes through vetted, stable APIs. This clear separation of concerns protects invariants, simplifies maintenance, and paves the way for safe extension as our application grows.

Summary

So, to sum up our understanding, we learned to model tasks as a **Task** data class with read-only and mutable properties, ensuring each instance carried its own identity, description, priority flag, completion status, and creation timestamp. We then used the primary constructor for concise property initialization and added secondary constructors to support alternate creation paths—parsing raw strings or scheduling due-date tasks—while centralizing validation in **init** blocks.

Next, we then defined a **CommandHandler** interface and concrete handler classes, then dispatched commands polymorphically, replacing brittle **when** chains with a flexible list of handlers. We abstracted shared behavior into an abstract base class, inheriting logging and error-handling logic and marking helper methods **protected** to restrict access. We hid internal state in **TaskService** by marking the task store and helper methods **private**, and exposed only read-only views via **toMap()**. We then applied **internal** visibility to module-specific utilities, preventing external misuse. All of these object-oriented techniques like classes, constructors, inheritance, interfaces, and encapsulation helped together to transform our Task Tracker app into a extensible system where new commands, storage backends, or features integrate seamlessly without risking internal invariants.

Chapter 6: Collection Handling and Iteration Patterns

Chapter Overview

Until now, we learned a lot. We now begin with declaring and manipulating dynamic lists to preserve task insertion order, appending IDs and iterating over them with **`for`** loops and **`withIndex()`**. We will explore fixed-capacity arrays, locating empty slots, storing tasks by index, and iterating over indices to display non-null entries.

Next, we will enforce uniqueness using **`MutableSet`** for descriptions and tags, using **`add()`** to prevent duplicates. Here, we will define and update a **`MutableMap<String, MutableList<Task>>`** to categorize tasks by status, demonstrating constant-time lookups and dynamic updates. After that, we will practice traversing collections with **`for`** loops over lists, arrays, and numeric ranges—using **`step`**, **`downTo`**, and **`indices`**—to process and display tasks sequentially. Finally, we will unlock declarative pipelines by applying **`filter`**, **`map`**, **`groupBy`**, and **`flatMap`** to select, transform, and group tasks, creating summary lists, CSV exports, and category reports. By the end of this chapter, we will be able to command both imperative and functional collection techniques to manage, traverse, and transform task data in our application.

Managing Lists and Arrays

So far, we have seen how maps associate task IDs with **`Task`** objects, but many scenarios call for ordered, sequential data structures. The Lists and arrays provide that order: **`List<T>`** and **`Array<T>`** let us store elements in a specific sequence, iterate by index, and enjoy built-in operations such as filtering, mapping, and slicing. In Kotlin, an immutable **`List<T>`** exposes read-only operations—no additions or removals—while **`MutableList<T>`** lets us change the contents dynamically. Arrays, by contrast, are fixed in size once created; we use **`Array<T>`** or specialized variants like **`IntArray`** to hold a predetermined number of elements. Each choice balances flexibility, performance, and intent: use lists when we expect to grow or shrink collections at runtime, arrays when we know capacity ahead of time or need tight control over memory layout. Throughout our app project, we will leverage lists to record insertion order, support undo stacks, and maintain history logs, and we will experiment with arrays for fixed-capacity storage or performance comparisons.

MutableList for Dynamic Task Sequences

Here, you begin by declaring a **`MutableList`** to track task IDs in the order they were added. Alongside our **`tasks`** map, we add:

```
// Tracks insertion order for tasks
private val insertionOrder: MutableList<Int> = mutableListOf()
```

When a task is created, we append its ID to this list:

```
fun handleAdd(args: String) {
    val task = Task(nextId, args.trim())
    service.addTask(task)
    insertionOrder.add(nextId)          // record the order
    println("Task added: $task")
    nextId++
}
```

By maintaining **insertionOrder**, we enable features such as undoing the last addition or replaying tasks in chronological sequence. Now, to display tasks in the order added rather than by ID sorting, we write:

```
fun handleListByOrder() {
    if (insertionOrder.isEmpty()) {
        println("No tasks found.")
    } else {
        insertionOrder.forEach { id ->
            val task = service.getTask(id)
            println("$id: ${task.description}")
        }
    }
}
```

Here, we replaced the **tasks.entries.joinToString** approach with index-based iteration over **insertionOrder**, preserving the exact sequence of user actions. Because **MutableList** grows dynamically, we never worry about running out of capacity when users add an arbitrary number of tasks.

The use of **MutableList** also simplifies implementing undo or redo patterns. For example, to remove the most recently added task, we write:

```
fun handleUndo() {
    if (insertionOrder.isNotEmpty()) {
```

```
        val lastId =
insertionOrder.removeAt(insertionOrder.lastIndex)
        service.removeTask(lastId)
        println("Undid task $lastId")
    } else println("Nothing to undo.")
}
```

This code clearly communicates intent: take the last element and remove both from the history list and the task repository.

Arrays for Fixed-Capacity Storage

Suppose we want to limit our app to a maximum of 100 entries for performance or memory reasons. An array provides a fixed buffer we can index directly. At the top of **`Main.kt`**, declare:

```
private const val MAX_TASKS = 100
private val taskArray: Array<Task?> = arrayOfNulls(MAX_TASKS)
```

Each slot in **`taskArray`** initially holds **`null`**. When adding a task, we find the first empty slot:

```
fun handleAdd(args: String) {
    val index = taskArray.indexOfFirst { it == null }
    if (index != -1) {
        val task = Task(nextId, args.trim())
        taskArray[index] = task
        insertionOrder.add(nextId)
        println("Task added at slot $index: $task")
        nextId++
    } else println("Task limit of $MAX_TASKS reached.")
}
```

In the above, the **`indexOfFirst`** returns the position of the first **`null`**, letting we place the new task without scanning the entire map. This approach trades dynamic resizing for faster slot lookup in predictable memory.

When listing tasks via the array, we loop through indices and skip **`null`**:

```
fun handleListArray() {
    taskArray.forEachIndexed { i, task ->
        task?.let { println("[$i] ${it.id}:
${it.description}") }
    }
}
```

By using **forEachIndexed**, we gain both the index and the element in the lambda, letting we display the slot number alongside task details. This pattern demonstrates how arrays support positional semantics that differ from list iteration.

Lists and Arrays Conversion

Now here, you may need to move data between arrays and lists. The Kotlin offers **toTypedArray()** on **List<T>** and **toList()** on **Array<T>** (or **toList()** on primitive arrays via specialized functions).

For example, to capture the current insertion order as an array of IDs:

```
val orderArray: Array<Int> = insertionOrder.toTypedArray()
orderArray.forEach { println("Ordered ID: $it") }
```

And conversely, to seed a list from the first ten slots of **taskArray**, we write:

```
val firstTenTasks: List<Task> = taskArray.sliceArray(0 until
10)
    .mapNotNull { it }
firstTenTasks.forEach { println("Preview: ${it.id} ->
${it.description}") }
```

With the use of **sliceArray** and **mapNotNull**, we can extract a subarray and remove empty slots. This interconversion flexibility helps us choose the right tool for each context while reusing data safely.

We now control both dynamic and fixed-size data structures in our app. This is because we have mastered lists and arrays. This enables ordered iteration, slot management, and efficient data access patterns. Our application becomes both adaptable for general use and optimized for situations where predictability and performance are important.

Organizing Storage using Sets and Maps

We have used lists and arrays to maintain ordered sequences of tasks, but many requirements call for collections that enforce uniqueness or associate keys with values. A **Set<T>** ensures that each element appears only once, perfect for tracking which task descriptions have been seen or which tags a user has applied. A **Map<K, V>** pairs keys with values, letting we look up tasks by custom identifiers, group tasks by status, or cache results for fast retrieval. In Kotlin, immutable interfaces (**Set<T>** and **Map<K, V>**) expose read-only operations, while **MutableSet<T>** and **MutableMap<K, V>** let us change contents dynamically. By choosing the right collection type, we express our intent clearly—"I want no duplicates" or "I need key-based lookup"—and gain efficient storage and retrieval semantics for our app.

Tracking Unique Descriptions with MutableSet

Let us say that we want to prevent duplicate task descriptions. We declare a **MutableSet<String>** to record each description as it arrives:

```
private val uniqueDescriptions: MutableSet<String> =
mutableSetOf()
```

For this, inside our **"add"** handler, we check and update the set:

```
fun handleAdd(args: String) {
    val desc = args.trim()
    if (uniqueDescriptions.add(desc)) {
        val task = Task(nextId, desc)
        service.addTask(task)
        insertionOrder.add(nextId)
        println("Task added: $task")
        nextId++
    } else {
        println("Duplicate description ignored.")
    }
}
```

In the above, the **add(desc)** returns **true** only if **desc** was not already present. When a duplicate is entered, we inform the user and skip creation. This pattern uses **MutableSet**'s constant-time **add** and **contains** operations to enforce uniqueness with minimal overhead.

You can also use a set to manage tags that users apply to tasks. Define:

```
private val allTags: MutableSet<String> = mutableSetOf()
```

When a user tags a task—say **"tag 3 urgent"**—you parse the tag and update both the task's tag list and the global set:

```
fun handleTag(args: String) {
    val (idStr, tag) = args.split(" ", limit = 2).let { it[0]
to it.getOrNull(1).orEmpty() }
    val id = idStr.toIntOrNull()
    if (id != null && service.getTask(id) != null) {
        service.addTag(id, tag)
        allTags.add(tag)
        println("Added tag '$tag' to task $id")
    } else println("Invalid task ID or tag.")
}
```

Later, we can list all available tags quickly by iterating **allTags.forEach(::println)**.

Key-Value Pairing with MutableMap

Your core **tasks** store already uses a **MutableMap<Int, Task>**, letting we look up tasks by ID in constant time. To extend map usage for categorization, we might group tasks by status—pending, completed, or high priority.

For this, we declare:

```
private val tasksByStatus: MutableMap<String,
MutableList<Task>> = mutableMapOf(
    "Pending" to mutableListOf(),
    "Completed" to mutableListOf(),
    "HighPriority" to mutableListOf()
)
```

Whenever a task changes state, we update both the main **tasks** map and this status map. For example, in **handleAdd**:

```
tasksByStatus["Pending"]?.add(task)
if (task.highPriority)
tasksByStatus["HighPriority"]?.add(task)
```

When a user marks a task complete:

```
fun handleComplete(args: String) {
    val id = args.toIntOrNull()
    val task = service.getTask(id)
    if (task != null && !task.completed) {
        task.completed = true
        tasksByStatus["Pending"]?.remove(task)
        tasksByStatus["Completed"]?.add(task)
        println("Task $id marked complete.")
    } else println("Invalid ID or already completed.")
}
```

The retrieval of tasks by status becomes as simple as **`tasksByStatus["Pending"]?.forEach(::println)`**, offering a clear separation of concerns between task storage and categorized views.

Iterating Maps with 'forEach'

The Kotlin's **`Map`** interface provides **`forEach`** with a lambda that receives each key-value pair. In the below, we can destructure the pair for clarity:

```
tasks.forEach { (id, task) ->
    println("$id: ${task.description} [${task.status}]")
}
```

When iterating **`tasksByStatus`**, we can show category headings and their tasks:

```
tasksByStatus.forEach { (status, list) ->
    println("=== $status ===")
    list.forEach { println("${it.id}: ${it.description}") }
```

```
}
```

This nested iteration reads like a structured report, grouping tasks by key and listing related values.

'mapKeys' and 'mapValues'

If we need a transformed view without altering the original map, Kotlin's **mapKeys** and **mapValues** help. Suppose we want a map of IDs to descriptions only:

```
val idToDesc: Map<Int, String> = tasks.mapValues {
it.value.description }
```

Or we want to uppercase all status keys for display:

```
val upperStatusMap: Map<String, List<Task>> =
tasksByStatus.mapKeys { it.key.uppercase() }
```

These functions return new maps, preserving immutability of the originals while letting we adapt data for specific contexts.

Handling Missing Keys with 'getOrDefault' and 'getOrPut'

When updating maps, we often check if a key exists or provide a fallback. Kotlin offers:

- **getOrDefault(key, defaultValue)** returns **defaultValue** when key is absent.
- **getOrPut(key) { defaultValue }** returns existing value or inserts & returns the result of the lambda.

Now here, to add a tag list per task ID without pre-initializing all entries, we write:

```
private val tagsByTask: MutableMap<Int, MutableList<String>> =
mutableMapOf()

fun handleTag(args: String) {

    val (idStr, tag) = args.split(" ", limit = 2).let { it[0]
to it.getOrNull(1).orEmpty() }

    val id = idStr.toIntOrNull()

    if (id != null && service.getTask(id) != null) {

        val tagList = tagsByTask.getOrPut(id) {
mutableListOf() }

        if (tagList.add(tag)) println("Tagged task $id with
$tag")
```

```
        else println("Task $id already has tag $tag")
    } else println("Invalid ID.")
}
```

getOrPut ensures we never encounter **NullPointerException** when adding to a nested collection.

So overall, we now categorize tasks efficiently—enforcing uniqueness of descriptions and tags, grouping tasks by status or date, and performing key-based lookups with constant-time performance. These patterns equip our app to handle growing complexity while maintaining organized, intention-revealing code.

'For' Loops for Data Traversal

So far, we rely on sequential processing whenever we work with ordered collections. The Kotlin's **for** loop lets us traverse arrays, lists, ranges, and other iterable types with concise syntax. At its simplest, we write **for (element in collection) { ... }**, and the loop body runs once for each item. Under the hood, Kotlin calls the collection's iterator, fetching elements until no more remain. This pattern abstracts away index management and boundary checks, so we focus on the logic we want to apply, not on counter increments or overflow errors. When we need the position alongside the element, Kotlin offers **for ((index, element) in collection.withIndex())**. We can also iterate numeric ranges—**for (i in 1..10)**—or step through them with **step** or reverse them with **downTo**.

Iterating over List Collections

We are so far maintaining a **MutableList<Int>** called **insertionOrder** to reflect the order tasks were added. To display tasks in that exact sequence, we use a **for** loop:

```
fun handleListByOrder() {
    if (insertionOrder.isEmpty()) {
        println("No tasks found.")
    } else {
        for (id in insertionOrder) {
            val task = service.getTask(id)
            println("$id: ${task?.description}")
        }
    }
```

```
}
```

This loop emphasizes readability: we iterate **id** by name, fetch the corresponding **Task**, then display its description. Because **for** handles iteration for you, there's no need to check **insertionOrder.size** or manage an index variable.

When we want both the position in the list and the value—perhaps to number tasks differently—you use **withIndex()**:

```
for ((position, id) in insertionOrder.withIndex()) {
    val task = service.getTask(id)
    println("${position + 1}. [ID:$id] ${task?.description}")
}
```

In the above, the **withIndex()** yields **IndexedValue** pairs, and we destructure them into **position** and **id**. This pattern eliminates manual index tracking (**var i = 0**), making code more concise and less error-prone.

Traversing Array Elements by Index and Slot

When we stored tasks in a fixed-size **Array<Task?>** named **taskArray**, we work with slots that may be empty. To iterate by index, we use **forEachIndexed**, which provides both index and element:

```
fun handleListArray() {
    for ((slot, task) in taskArray.withIndex()) {
        if (task != null) {
            println("Slot $slot: ${task.id} ->
${task.description}")
        }
    }
}
```

Alternatively, to manipulate slots directly, we can loop over indices:

```
for (i in taskArray.indices) {
    val task = taskArray[i]
```

```
    if (task != null) println("[$i] ${task.id}: 
${task.description}")
}
```

The use of **taskArray.indices** removes magic numbers and automatically adapts if the array size changes. We avoid out-of-bounds errors and keep our loops robust against future capacity adjustments.

Numeric Ranges for Fixed Iterations

Beyond collections, we may also need to run code a fixed number of times or within numeric bounds. Kotlin supports ranges:

```
for (i in 1..5) { println("Countdown: $i") }
for (i in 10 downTo 1 step 2) { println("Even step: $i") }
for (i in 0 until insertionOrder.size) { println("Index $i → 
ID ${insertionOrder[i]}") }
```

Here, we might also preview only the first three tasks:

```
for (i in 0 until minOf(3, insertionOrder.size)) {
    val id = insertionOrder[i]
    println("Top ${i+1}: ${service.getTask(id)?.description}")
}
```

This loop ensures we never exceed the list's length and cleanly expresses "iterate three times or less.

Conditions within Loops

For advanced traversal, we can include **if** inside a loop or combine ranges and collections. For example, to print only high-priority tasks by order:

```
for (id in insertionOrder) {
    val task = service.getTask(id) ?: continue
    if (task.highPriority) println("! ${task.id}: 
${task.description}")
}
```

Using **continue**, we skip non-priority tasks without deep nesting. The loop remains straightforward: iterate, retrieve, check, and act.

Knowing the **for** loop variants—collection iteration, indexed traversal, and numeric ranges—you will write Task Tracker code that processes sequences succinctly, avoids common pitfalls, and expresses our intentions directly.

Filtering and Mapping Data

So far, we have learned the basics of using lists, sets, and maps in our app. Now we will unlock the true power of Kotlin's standard library by leveraging higher-order operations—**filter**, **map**, **flatMap**, **groupBy**—to transform collections declaratively. Rather than writing manual loops with **if** statements and accumulating results, we compose concise chains of operations that read like a data pipeline. Each step—filtering or mapping—returns a new collection, leaving the original intact. This immutability-first approach ensures predictable behavior and simplifies reasoning: we see exactly which elements flow into each stage. In our app, we will filter tasks by priority, completion status, or matching keywords; then map tasks to summary strings, CSV lines, or export formats. We will group tasks by categories, flatten nested tag lists, and combine operations to create powerful one-liners that replace dozens of lines of imperative code.

Filtering Tasks by Conditions

The filtering extracts only those elements that satisfy a predicate. In our app, we maintain a **Map<Int,Task>** called **tasks**. To show only high-priority tasks, we write:

```
val highPriorityTasks: Map<Int, Task> = tasks.filterValues {
it.highPriority }

if (highPriorityTasks.isEmpty()) {

    println("No high-priority tasks.")

} else {

    highPriorityTasks.forEach { (id, t) -> println("$id:
${t.description}") }

}
```

Within the lambda **{ it.highPriority }**, **it** refers to each **Task**. **filterValues** preserves the map's keys and values, returning a new **Map** containing only those entries. We avoid manual loops and **if** checks, achieving the same result in a single line.

To filter by keyword in the description—case-insensitively—you compose:

```
val keyword = "report"
```

```
val matching = tasks.filterValues {
    it.description.contains(keyword, ignoreCase = true)
}
println("Tasks matching '$keyword':")
matching.forEach { (id, t) -> println("$id: ${t.description}")
}
```

The swapping helps to reuse **filterValues** across multiple filters—priority, status, or text patterns—without rewriting loop logic.

Mapping Tasks to New Forms

The mapping transforms each element of a collection into a new form, producing a list of results. Let us say that we need a list of summary strings for export:

```
val summaries: List<String> = tasks.map { (id, t) ->
    "Task $id: ${t.description.take(30).let { if
(t.description.length > 30) "$it…" else it }}"
}
summaries.forEach(::println)
```

In the above, the **map** operates on the **Map**'s entries, destructuring each **(id, t)** pair. We build a formatted string, previewing the first 30 characters of each description, appending an ellipsis when necessary. The result is a **List<String>** of summaries, ideal for sending to a log or writing to a file.

When exporting to CSV, we map to lines with comma-separated values and escape quotes:

```
fun escapeCsv(value: String) = "\"${value.replace("\"",
"\"\"")}\""
val csvLines: List<String> = tasks.map { (id, t) ->
    listOf(id.toString(), escapeCsv(t.description),
t.status).joinToString(",")
}
println("ID,Description,Status")
csvLines.forEach(::println)
```

This pipeline covers escaping, joining, and mapping—all within a fluent chain.

Combining Filter and Map in Pipelines

Often, we filter first, then map the surviving elements. For example, to list only pending tasks as user-friendly messages:

```
tasks.filterValues { !it.completed }
     .map { (id, t) -> "Pending: $id — ${t.description}" }
     .forEach(::println)
```

This one-liner conveys intent immediately: "from tasks, pick those not completed, convert each to a formatted string, then print each." No temporary variables or loops obscure the flow.

If we need both keys and values, use **mapValues** to keep the map structure while transforming values:

```
val idToDesc: Map<Int, String> = tasks.mapValues {
it.value.description.uppercase() }
idToDesc.forEach { (id, desc) -> println("$id -> $desc") }
```

The **mapValues** leaves the keys untouched, returning a new **Map<Int, String>** that we can pass to other functions expecting that type.

Advanced Grouping and Flat-Mapping

Now here, to categorize tasks by status—Pending, Completed, HighPriority, we can simply use **groupBy**:

```
val grouped: Map<String, List<Task>> = tasks.values.groupBy {
task ->
    when {
        task.completed      -> "Completed"
        task.highPriority   -> "HighPriority"
        else                -> "Pending"
    }
}
grouped.forEach { (status, list) ->
    println("=== $status ===")
    list.forEach { println("${it.id}: ${it.description}") }
```

```
}
```

The **groupBy** returns a map whose keys are the category strings and whose values are lists of tasks in each category. This replaces manual population of **tasksByStatus**, centralizing grouping logic in one expressive call.

If our **Task** class included a list of tags—**tags: List<String>**, you could use **flatMap** to collect all tags across tasks into a single list:

```
val allTags: List<String> = tasks.values.flatMap { it.tags }
val uniqueTags = allTags.toSet()
println("Unique tags: $uniqueTags")
```

The **flatMap** maps each task to its **tags** list, then flattens the sublists into one master list. The conversion to a set then removes duplicates, giving we a quick tag inventory.

Summary

To quickly revise our lrarnings, we first introduced **MutableList** to track task insertion order, appending each new **Task** ID and iterating over the list to display tasks chronologically. We experimented with fixed-size **Array<Task?>**, locating empty slots via **indexOfFirst**, storing tasks by slot, and iterating by index to show occupied entries. We converted between lists and arrays using **toTypedArray()** and **sliceArray()**, demonstrating how to extract subcollections safely. We then created a **MutableSet<String>** to enforce unique task descriptions and tag collections, using **add()** to conditionally accept or reject duplicates. With **MutableMap<String, MutableList<Task>>**, we grouped tasks by status—Pending, Completed, HighPriority—updating the appropriate lists on state changes to support rapid category-based lookups.

We then applied **getOrPut** to manage nested maps like **tagsByTask**, ensuring tag lists initialized on demand. Numeric ranges and **for** loops processed fixed iterations and previewed slices of **insertionOrder**, utilizing **withIndex()**, **step**, **downTo**, and **until** for flexible traversal. Finally, we then adopted higher-order operations—**filterValues**, **map**, **groupBy**, **flatMap**—to declaratively select high-priority or keyword-matched tasks, transform tasks into summary strings or CSV lines, and group or flatten nested collections. Each of the collection type and operation was applied to the Task Tracker code, reinforcing how sequential, set, and mapping patterns yield concise, maintainable, and intention-revealing code for real-world needs.

Chapter 7: Managing Application State and Behavior

Chapter Overview

Here, in this chapter, we will begin with how we can represent application state using immutable data classes and confined mutable containers, enforcing contracts that keep our **`Task`** entities and ID generator predictable. Here, we will implement an observer interface and register console, logging, and reminder observers in our **`TaskService`** so that all interested components synchronize immediately when tasks are added, updated, or removed.

Next, we will then define operational modes with a sealed **`AppState`** hierarchy—Running, ReadOnly, Maintenance—and learn to guard command execution through explicit state checks or a shared **`withState`** helper. We will be introduced to feature flags such as **`autoSaveEnabled`** and tie them into our mutating methods to conditionally persist changes. Finally, we will enhance the user interface by reflecting current state in the REPL prompt and by providing commands to switch modes and toggle flags. By the time we reach the end of this chapter, we will have a sturdy, responsive state management system that leads to logical, context-aware behavior throughout our app.

Understanding Mutable and Immutable States

Every app's functionality depends on the data it holds and how that data changes over time. State management is all about organizing, tracking, and updating that data. It helps our app behave predictably, even when users are interacting with it. In a command-line Task Tracker, state includes the list of tasks, each task's completion flag, priority status, and any configuration toggles such as reminder settings. If we let the state change without limits—like any code updating **`tasks`** or **`nextId`** without boundaries—you risk data races, inconsistent displays, and bugs that are hard to reproduce. If we think about which parts of our state can't change and which ones can, we'll have a better understanding. Data that can't change prevents accidental changes and makes it easier to reason, while things that can change let us deal with behavior that's always changing. Good state management balances all these factors, making sure that only the right code paths perform updates and that we can trace every change back to a single, well-defined source.

Immutable State with Data Classes and Snapshots

Here in Kotlin, the data classes are excellent for representing immutable snapshots of state. Once we create an instance, its **`val`** properties never change. For example, our **`Task`** class had **`val id`**, **`val description`**, and **`val createdTimestamp`**. We treated **`completed`** as **`var`** previously, but we can instead model each task's state transition by producing a new instance via **`copy()`**, leaving the original untouched. This approach encourages us to think in terms of state snapshots.

To do this, we go to **`TaskService`**, and replace in-place mutation of **`completed`** with:

```
fun markComplete(id: Int) {
    val old = tasks[id] ?: return
    val updated = old.copy(completed = true)
    tasks[id] = updated
}
```

In the above, we treat **`tasks`**—a **`MutableMap<Int, Task>`**—as the single mutable reference, but each **`Task`** remains immutable. This pattern ensures that any code holding a reference to the old **`Task`** sees the original state, and any new reads fetch the updated snapshot. We avoid unintended side-effects in functions that merely read tasks.

When we need to present the entire state—say, printing a report—you can take an immutable snapshot of the map and pass it around safely:

```
fun snapshotTasks(): Map<Int, Task> = tasks.toMap()
```

The other modules consume this read-only view without fear of mutation.

Mutable State with Explicit Constructs

Sometimes, our application demands true mutability—counters that increment, flags that toggle, or caches that update in place. Kotlin offers **`var`** for variables that change reference, and mutable collections—**`MutableList`**, **`MutableMap`**, **`MutableSet`**—for dynamic contents. In **`Main.kt`**, we maintain **`var nextId`** as a mutable integer generator. We also have a **`MutableMap<Int, Task>`** and a **`MutableList<Int>`** for insertion order. When we add a task, we explicitly mutate these constructs:

```
val id = nextId++
tasks[id] = Task(id, desc)
insertionOrder.add(id)
```

By confining these mutability points to a single service class or module, we know exactly where and when changes occur. We avoid scattering **`var`** declarations throughout our code, which could lead to state inconsistencies.

If we introduce a feature flag—such as enabling periodic reminders—you might declare:

```
var remindersEnabled: Boolean = true
```

Because this flag genuinely toggles at runtime, we choose **`var`**. In our reminder loop, we check this flag each cycle:

```
while (remindersEnabled) {
    // send reminders
    delay(60_000)
}
```

This explicit mutability contrasts with our immutable **Task** instances, highlighting where state is meant to evolve.

Blending Immutable and Mutable Approaches

We maintain a single mutable **tasks** map to hold the latest snapshots of each task, and we update entries only through controlled methods in **TaskService**. Each **Task** object remains immutable, so reading modules never see half-updated state. Our ID generator and feature flags use **var** where practical, but we group them in a single location. When presenting data, we convert mutable collections to immutable views—**tasks.toMap()**, **insertionOrder.toList()**—before passing to display functions. This practice ensures that once a view is generated, it cannot change unexpectedly during rendering or logging.

For example, in our **"list"** command, we write:

```
fun handleList() {
    val snapshot = service.snapshotTasks().toList()
    snapshot.forEach { (_, t) ->
        println("${t.id}: ${t.description} [${t.status}]")
    }
}
```

You call **toList()** on the map's entries to freeze the state at that instant. Even if another thread or background job updates **tasks**, our listing remains consistent from start to finish.

The idea is to use permanent snapshots and clearly defined temporary constructs. This will help us keep track of task status and application behavior, creating a solid foundation for the reactive and event-driven patterns that we'll cover next.

Propagating State across Application Components

We have learned to confine mutable state inside **TaskService**—tasks map, ID generator, feature flags—but a real-world application comprises multiple modules, such as command handlers, UI layers, background jobs, and persistence adapters. When a user adds, updates, or removes a task, every interested component must receive that change to stay in sync. If our reminder scheduler, CLI output, and audit logger operate on stale data, we risk inconsistent behavior and confusing user experience. The propagating state changes ensures that all parts of our app react immediately and coherently to user actions, maintaining a unified view of the application.

Defining Observer Contract

Here, we implement a simple observer pattern. First, declare an interface that all listeners must follow. In **TaskService.kt**, define:

```
interface TaskObserver {
    fun onTaskAdded(task: Task)
    fun onTaskUpdated(task: Task)
    fun onTaskRemoved(taskId: Int)
}
```

This contract specifies three callbacks. Any component interested in state changes implements one or more of these methods.

Registering Observers

Inside **TaskService**, we maintain a list of observers and provide registration methods. We add the following to **TaskService.kt**:

```
private val observers: MutableList<TaskObserver> =
mutableListOf()
fun addObserver(observer: TaskObserver) {
    observers.add(observer)
}
fun removeObserver(observer: TaskObserver) {
    observers.remove(observer)
}
```

This encapsulates these lists as **private**, thereby we guarantee that only **TaskService** controls who receives notifications.

Notifying Observers on State Changes

Whenever state mutates like adding, copying on update, or removing, it invoke the relevant callbacks. So here, we refactor our methods:

```
fun addTask(task: Task): Int {
    tasks[task.id] = task
    save()
    observers.forEach { it.onTaskAdded(task) }
    return task.id
}
fun markComplete(id: Int) {
    val old = tasks[id] ?: return
    val updated = old.copy(completed = true)
    tasks[id] = updated
    save()
    observers.forEach { it.onTaskUpdated(updated) }
}
fun removeTask(id: Int): Boolean {
    val removed = tasks.remove(id) != null
    if (removed) {
        save()
        observers.forEach { it.onTaskRemoved(id) }
    }
    return removed
}
```

By doing this, each mutation now triggers notifications immediately after persistence, ensuring that every observer sees the latest state.

Building CLI Observer for Real-Time Display

To refresh the console view as tasks change, we implement a **TaskObserver** that prints updates:

```
class ConsoleObserver : TaskObserver {
    override fun onTaskAdded(task: Task) {
        println(">>> [Observer] Task added: ${task.id} ->
${task.description}")
    }
    override fun onTaskUpdated(task: Task) {
        println(">>> [Observer] Task updated: ${task.id}
completed=${task.completed}")
    }
    override fun onTaskRemoved(taskId: Int) {
        println(">>> [Observer] Task removed: $taskId")
    }
}
```

We first register it at startup in **Main.kt**:

```
val service = TaskService(JsonFileRepository("tasks.json"))
val consoleObserver = ConsoleObserver()
service.addObserver(consoleObserver)
```

Now, when we execute **add**, **complete**, or **remove** commands, we immediately see observer messages interleaved with our normal output, confirming that state propagation works.

Logging Observer for Audit Trails

You may need to record every state change to a file for audit or undo functionality. To do this, we create a **LoggingObserver**:

```
class LoggingObserver(private val logPath: String) :
TaskObserver {
    override fun onTaskAdded(task: Task) {
        File(logPath).appendText("ADDED:
${task.id},${task.description}\n")
    }
    override fun onTaskUpdated(task: Task) {
```

```
        File(logPath).appendText("UPDATED:
${task.id},completed=${task.completed}\n")
    }
    override fun onTaskRemoved(taskId: Int) {
        File(logPath).appendText("REMOVED: $taskId\n")
    }
}
```

In **Main.kt**, we then register it alongside the console observer:

```
service.addObserver(LoggingObserver("audit.log"))
```

Now every mutation appends a line to **audit.log**, giving we a permanent record of operations.

Background Reminder Observer

Here, we combine state propagation with our reminder loop. Rather than polling the **tasks** map, we push updates to a **ReminderObserver** that tracks due dates:

```
class ReminderObserver(private val channel: Channel<Task>) :
TaskObserver {
    override fun onTaskAdded(task: Task) {
        if (!task.completed) channel.offer(task)
    }
    override fun onTaskUpdated(task: Task) {
        if (task.completed) channel.remove { it.id == task.id
}
    }
    override fun onTaskRemoved(taskId: Int) {
        channel.remove { it.id == taskId }
    }
}
```

In our coroutine setup:

```
val reminderChannel = Channel<Task>(Channel.UNLIMITED)
```

```
val reminderObserver = ReminderObserver(reminderChannel)
service.addObserver(reminderObserver)
GlobalScope.launch {
    for (task in reminderChannel) {
        delay(60_000)
        println("Reminder: Task ${task.id} is still pending.")
    }
}
```

This reactive design pushes new tasks into the channel as they appear and removes them when they complete or are removed. Our background coroutine processes only current state, avoiding expensive periodic scans.

By propagating state through observers, we were able to decouple components while ensuring real-time synchronization. Tasks like command-line output, logging, and background jobs all remain in harmony as the Task Tracker's state evolves.

State-Based Logic for Operational Control

The truth about real-world applications is that they need logic that can adapt behavior based on the current state and context. They don't just need simple add, remove, or update operations. With state-based logic, you write conditional code that checks one or more state variables before proceeding. This makes sure that operations happen only when they're valid and prevents any unexpected side-effects. You can make business rules more predictable and user-friendly by putting them in writing. For example, you could say that you don't allow task additions when storage is full or that you don't allow removals during batch operations. Plus, centralizing state checks keeps our handlers lean: each command first verifies preconditions, then executes core logic, and finally updates state. This pattern makes our app stronger and more resistant to misuse, as well as easier to expand as new requirements come up.

Modeling Operational Modes with Sealed Classes

One way to implement state-based control is to define discrete operational modes. In **State.kt**, we then create:

```
sealed class AppState {
    object Running       : AppState()
    object ReadOnly      : AppState()
```

```
    object Maintenance  : AppState()
}
```

Here,

- ***Running***: normal operations—add, remove, list.
- ***ReadOnly***: additions and removals disabled, listing allowed.
- ***Maintenance***: only removal of all tasks permitted.

In **TaskService**, we then add a mutable property to track mode:

```
var state: AppState = AppState.Running
    private set
fun setState(newState: AppState) { state = newState }
```

The private setter ensures only **TaskService** changes mode, preserving encapsulation.

Guarding Handlers with State Checks

Now before executing command logic, each handler verifies the current **state**. In **AddHandler**:

```
override fun execute(args: String) {
    if (service.state != AppState.Running) {
        println("Cannot add tasks while in ${service.state}
mode.")
        return
    }
    // existing add logic…
}
```

In **RemoveHandler**:

```
override fun execute(args: String) {
    when (service.state) {
        AppState.Running, AppState.Maintenance -> {
            // allow removal
            handleRemove(args)
```

```
        }
        AppState.ReadOnly -> println("Removal disabled in
read-only mode.")
    }
}
```

By front-loading state checks, we prevent invalid operations early, reducing nested **if** blocks inside core logic.

Toggling Modes via Commands

It gives users commands to switch modes. We can define **ModeHandler**:

```
class ModeHandler(private val service: TaskService) :
CommandHandler {
    override val commandName = "mode"
    override fun execute(args: String) {
        val mode = args.trim().lowercase()
        service.setState(when (mode) {
            "running"      -> AppState.Running
            "readonly"     -> AppState.ReadOnly
            "maintenance"  -> AppState.Maintenance
            else           -> {
                println("Unknown mode: $mode")
                return
            }
        })
        println("State set to ${service.state}")
    }
}
```

This registers **ModeHandler** like other handlers. Now, typing **mode readonly** immediately prevents additions and removals, illustrating dynamic behavior control.

Combining Feature Flags and State Checks

Beyond modes, we use Boolean flags to gate specific features. Suppose we introduce a flag **autoSaveEnabled**. In **TaskService**:

```
var autoSaveEnabled: Boolean = true
fun saveIfNeeded() {
    if (autoSaveEnabled) save()
}
```

In each mutating method, we then replace direct **save()** calls with **saveIfNeeded()**. The users can toggle autosave with **autosave on|off** commands, implemented via a handler:

```
class AutoSaveHandler(private val service: TaskService) :
CommandHandler {
    override val commandName = "autosave"
    override fun execute(args: String) {
        service.autoSaveEnabled = (args.trim().lowercase() ==
"on")
        println("Auto-save ${if (service.autoSaveEnabled)
"enabled" else "disabled"}.")
    }
}
```

This conditional save behavior demonstrates how feature flags complement mode checks, enabling fine-grained operational control.

Centralizing Preconditions in Helper

To avoid repeating state checks in each handler, we then define a higher-order function in **TaskService**:

```
fun withState(vararg allowed: AppState, action: () -> Unit) {
    if (state in allowed) action()
    else println("Operation not allowed in $state mode.")
}
```

The handlers then simplify to:

```
override fun execute(args: String) {
    service.withState(AppState.Running) {
        handleAdd(args)
    }
}
```

This pattern encapsulates state-based gating in one place, boosting code reuse and clarity.

Dynamic UI Prompts Based on State

For a more interactive CLI, we adjust the prompts to reflect state. To do this, in our main loop:

```
while (true) {
    print("[${service.state}]> ")
    val input = readLine().orEmpty().trim()
    // parsing and dispatch…
}
```

The users immediately see the current mode in the prompt, reducing confusion about which commands will succeed.

By embedding state-based logic through sealed modes, feature flags, and centralized precondition checks, our app adapts smoothly to user actions and configuration changes.

Summary

To quickly summarize, we learned to treat each **`Task`** as an immutable snapshot by using **`data class`** and **`copy()`** for updates, ensuring that only the **`tasks`** map itself remained mutable. We confined all mutable state—ID counters, feature flags, and the tasks map—within **`TaskService`**, exposing only controlled methods and read-only snapshots to callers. We then implemented an observer pattern by defining **`TaskObserver`**, registering observers in **`TaskService`**, and notifying them on additions, updates, and removals. We then built concrete observers—console logging, audit-file logging, and a reminder channel—that synchronized their behavior in real time with state changes.

Later, we modeled operational modes with a sealed **`AppState`** hierarchy and guarded each command handler with state checks or a shared **`withState`** helper, enabling read-only, maintenance, and running modes. We successfully introduced feature flags like **`autoSaveEnabled`** and toggled behavior dynamically. We then refined our main loop prompt to display current mode, enhancing user awareness. Through these practices—immutable snapshots, confined mutability, observer notifications, sealed-state gating, and feature-flag checks—we were able to ensure that our app's behavior adapted smoothly to user actions and configuration changes.

CHAPTER 8: FUNCTIONAL PROGRAMMING WITH LAMBDAS

Chapter Overview

This chapter is going to start with a look at lambda syntax in Kotlin. You'll learn how to define anonymous functions using curly braces, arrows, and the implicit **`it`** parameter, and how inline functions improve performance by inlining lambda bodies.

Next, we will apply lambdas to collection manipulation: using **`filter`**, **`map`**, **`fold`**, and **`flatMap`** to select, transform, and aggregate **`Task`** objects in concise pipelines without manual loops. We will create extension functions to name and reuse transformation steps, improving readability. Then, we will explore function chaining and composition, linking multiple lambdas into fluent data-processing pipelines that sort, group, and combine task data, and leverage **`onEach`** for in-line side-effects. Finally, we will integrate lambdas into event handling, defining a helper to register inline callbacks for task additions, updates, and removals, and build asynchronous, reactive flows with coroutines, **`SharedFlow`**, and channels.

By the time we reach the end of the chapter, we'll be using Kotlin's functional features to write clear, efficient, and scalable Task Tracker code. This code will react to state changes and data transformations with minimal boilerplate.

Lambda Syntax and Structure

We've already seen functions as first-class citizens in higher-order wrappers and observers, but lambda expressions take that concept further by embedding anonymous functions directly where we need them. When the logic is simple and there's only one instance of it, lambdas do away with the need for named helper methods. Our app lets us supply small bits of code to collection operations, event dispatchers, and utility functions without messing up our namespace. Lambdas make code easier to read by keeping behavior close to its context, getting rid of boilerplate class definitions for single-method interfaces, and letting us compose operations smoothly. Once we get lambda syntax and how it works with inline and extension functions, we'll be able to write task filtering, mapping, sorting, and callbacks in a clear, step-by-step way, instead of the more complex procedural style.

Basic Lambda Syntax

As learned previously, the lambda literal appears inside curly braces, with parameters (optional) on the left of **`->`** and the body on the right. For example, a predicate checking even numbers looks like:

```
val isEven: (Int) -> Boolean = { number -> number % 2 == 0 }
```

When a lambda has exactly one parameter, we can use the implicit **`it`** name:

```
val isOdd: (Int) -> Boolean = { it % 2 != 0 }
```

In the above, the **it** represents the single **Int** passed in, shaving off extra syntax.

Omitting Parentheses for Trailing Lambdas

If a function's last parameter is a function type, we can move the lambda outside the parentheses. For example, calling **filter** on a list of tasks:

```
val urgentTasks = tasks.filterValues { it.highPriority }
```

Under the hood, the **filterValues** is declared as **fun <K,V> Map<K,V>.filterValues(predicate: (V)->Boolean): Map<K,V>**. Because **predicate** is last, we write the lambda after the method call, improving readability.

Inline Lambdas and Performance Benefits

If we mark our higher-order functions with **inline**, we tell the compiler to copy lambda bytecode directly at the call site, eliminating the cost of creating function objects. For instance:

```
inline fun <T> measure(name: String, block: () -> T): T {
    val start = System.nanoTime()
    val result = block()
    println("$name took ${(System.nanoTime()-
start)/1_000_000}ms")
    return result
}
```

When we invoke **measure("filtering") { tasks.filterValues { it.completed } }**, no additional allocation occurs for the outer or inner lambdas, keeping performance tight even in loops or hot code paths.

Destructuring Lambdas for Clarity

When operating on maps or indexed lists, we often need both key and value or index and element. The lambdas support destructuring directly in the parameter list:

```
tasks.forEach { (id, task) ->
    println("$id: ${task.description}")
```

```
}
```

or

```
insertionOrder.withIndex().forEach { (index, id) ->
    println("${index+1}. Task ID $id")
}
```

The destructuring eliminates manual unpacking inside the body, focusing on the logic rather than boilerplate.

Quick Hands-On with Lambdas

Filtering and Mapping in One Line

You can combine **`filterValues`** and **`map`** to select and transform tasks in a single expression:

```
val pendingDescriptions: List<String> = tasks
    .filterValues { !it.completed }
    .map { (_, t) -> t.description }
```

This chain yields a list of pending task descriptions without any mutable accumulation.

Sorting with Lambdas

To list tasks by creation time in descending order, use:

```
val recentTasks = tasks.values
    .sortedByDescending { it.createdTimestamp }
    .take(5)
for (task in recentTasks) println("${task.id}:
${task.description}")
```

`sortedByDescending { it.createdTimestamp }` expresses sorting intent directly.

Inline Callbacks for Event Handling

When we registered observers, we used concrete classes. With lambdas, we can subscribe on the fly for one-off behavior:

```
service.addObserver(object : TaskObserver {
```

```
    override fun onTaskAdded(task: Task) {
        println("Lambda observer: task ${task.id} added")
    }
    // other methods omitted for brevity
})
```

You can simplify this with a helper accepting lambdas for each callback:

```
fun TaskService.onTaskEvents(
    added: (Task) -> Unit = {},
    updated: (Task) -> Unit = {},
    removed: (Int)  -> Unit = {}
) {
    addObserver(object : TaskObserver {
        override fun onTaskAdded(task: Task)   = added(task)
        override fun onTaskUpdated(task: Task) = updated(task)
        override fun onTaskRemoved(id: Int)    = removed(id)
    })
}
service.onTaskEvents(
    added   = { println(">>> Added ${it.id}") },
    removed = { id -> println(">>> Removed $id") }
)
```

This pattern uses lambdas to inject only the behavior we need, without defining separate listener classes.

After practicing the lambda syntax—parameter declarations, **`it`** shorthand, trailing lambdas, destructuring, and inline functions—you will remove boilerplate, concentrate logic where it belongs, and create expressive, maintainable Task Tracker code that reads like a series of clear data transformations.

Collection Manipulation using Lambdas

Integrating Inline Functions with Lambdas

So far, we have seen how inline higher-order functions like **`measure`** reduce allocation overhead by copying lambda bodies at call sites. Now we apply that principle to collection operations. In Kotlin, functions such as **`filter`**, **`map`**, **`fold`**, and **`reduce`** are already marked **`inline`**, so every lambda we pass to them in our app executes with minimal runtime cost. When we write

```
val urgentTasks = tasks.values.filter { it.highPriority }
```

the **`filter`** call inlines our predicate **`{ it.highPriority }`** directly, avoiding the creation of a **`Function1`** object. This tight integration means we can chain operations—filtering, mapping, sorting—without worrying about performance. In our application, we will use these inline lambdas to sculpt task collections into the exact shape we need: selecting items that match criteria, transforming them into summaries or export formats, and aggregating data such as counts or timestamps.

Filtering Tasks with Lambdas

Rather than iterating manually and appending matching tasks to a new list, we write concise filter expressions. Suppose we want only incomplete, high-priority tasks that contain the word "report." We compose:

```
val criticalReports = tasks.values
    .filter { !it.completed }
    .filter { it.highPriority }
    .filter { it.description.contains("report", ignoreCase =
true) }
```

Each **`filter`** call applies our lambda to every **`Task`** in turn, returning a new list. Because these methods are inline, there is no hidden overhead beyond the predicate itself. We then display the results with another lambda:

```
criticalReports.forEach { println("${it.id}:
${it.description}") }
```

With this, we express multi-step selection logic declaratively. Any change in criteria requires adjusting only one lambda, keeping our code DRY and focused solely on the conditions that matter to our app's business rules.

Mapping and Transforming Collections

Once we have filtered a collection, we often need to transform each element. Mapping lambdas let us convert a **Task** into any other form—a formatted string, a CSV line, or a simplified data class for export. For example, to prepare pending tasks for JSON serialization, we write:

```
val pendingJson = tasks.values
    .filter { !it.completed }
    .map { task ->
        """{ "id": ${task.id}, "desc": "${task.description}",
"time": ${task.createdTimestamp} }"""
    }
```

Each **map** lambda runs inline and returns a new **List<String>**. We then join lines for file output:

```
File("pending.json").writeText(pendingJson.joinToString(prefix
= "[", postfix = "]", separator = ","))
```

This pipeline replaces dozens of lines of loop logic with a clear, three-step chain: filter, map, write. The code reads like a description of our intent rather than procedural plumbing.

Reducing and Aggregating with Lambdas

Beyond one-to-one transformations, we can collapse collections into single values using **reduce** or **fold**. To compute the total number of completed tasks, we use:

```
val totalCompleted = tasks.values.count { it.completed }
```

But if we need more complex aggregation—say, summing estimated durations—you define a **duration** property on **Task** and write:

```
val totalEstimate = tasks.values
    .map { it.estimatedMinutes }
    .fold(0) { acc, minutes -> acc + minutes }
```

In the above, the **fold** takes an initial accumulator (**0**) and an inline lambda that adds each element. Because **fold** is inline, this numeric accumulation runs in a tight loop. We avoid mutable variables entirely, gaining thread-safe behavior if we later parallelize operations.

Crafting Pipelines for Batch Operations

The true power of inline lambdas emerges when we build multi-stage pipelines that both filter and transform. For archiving old tasks, we might write:

```
val archiveLines = tasks.values
    .filter {
Instant.ofEpochMilli(it.createdTimestamp).isBefore(Instant.now
().minus(30, ChronoUnit.DAYS)) }
    .map { task -> serialize(task) }
    .onEach { line -> File("archive.log").appendText(line +
"\n") }
```

onEach applies a side-effect inline without breaking the pipeline, letting we write file output cleanly between filter and map. This style keeps our app code expressive: each lambda focuses on a single operation, and the overall pipeline reads like a sequence of transformations and actions.

With hands-on through inline lambdas for collection manipulation like filtering, mapping, reducing, and piping, you are able to build highly readable, performant code that adapts seamlessly.

Function Chaining and Composition Techniques

You have learned how individual lambdas power filtering, mapping, and aggregation. Function chaining builds on that by linking multiple operations into a fluent pipeline, so data flows through each transformation step without intermediate variables or loops. In Kotlin, every collection operation—**filter**, **map**, **flatMap**, **onEach**, **groupBy**, **sortedBy**—returns a new collection or value, letting we invoke the next method directly. This style reads like a chain of commands: "from this collection, keep these elements, then convert them, then group them," mirroring our mental model of the data transformation. By composing small, focused functions, we avoid boilerplate, reduce cognitive load, and make each pipeline self-documenting.

Building a Simple Pipeline

So here, we start with a list of all **Task** objects. Suppose we need a list of descriptions for tasks that are high priority and pending, sorted by creation time. We write:

```
val pipeline = tasks.values
    .filter { it.highPriority && !it.completed }
    .sortedBy { it.createdTimestamp }
    .map { it.description }
```

In the above, the *filter* selects only tasks with both **highPriority** and not **completed**. The

sortedBy orders them from oldest to newest based on timestamp, and the ***map*** extracts the **`description`** string for each.

When we call **`pipeline.forEach(::println)`**, we see exactly those descriptions in order. This one-liner replaces nested loops, conditional checks, and temporary lists, making the logic transparent and maintainable.

Composing Custom Transformations

You can extract reusable transformations into extension functions and chain them. For example, define in **`TaskExtensions.kt`**:

```
fun Collection<Task>.pendingHighPriority(): List<Task> =
    filter { it.highPriority && !it.completed }
fun List<Task>.sortByCreation(): List<Task> =
    sortedBy { it.createdTimestamp }
```

Then our pipeline becomes:

```
tasks.values
    .pendingHighPriority()
    .sortByCreation()
    .map(Task::description)
    .forEach(::println)
```

By naming each stage, we clarify intent: we first narrow tasks to those both pending and critical, then sort them, then extract descriptions. The change of criteria or order requires editing only the corresponding extension, not the entire pipeline.

Flattening Nested Structures with 'flatMap'

When tasks include multiple tags (**`tags: List<String>`**), we often need to process all tags across tasks. Chaining **`flatMap`** with other operations produces concise results. To list unique tags used by pending tasks, we write:

```
val pendingTags: Set<String> = tasks.values
    .filter { !it.completed }
    .flatMap { it.tags }
    .toSet()
```

In the above, the ***filter*** limits tasks to those pending, the ***flatMap*** flattens each task's tag list into a single stream of tags, and the ***toSet*** removes duplicates. By chaining these lambdas, we avoid manual loops and maintain clarity on each transformation's responsibility.

Injecting Side-Effects with 'onEach'

Sometimes we want to observe data flowing through the pipeline without breaking it. The **onEach** operator executes a lambda for each element, then returns the unmodified collection. For real-time logging of tasks being processed, we chain:

```
tasks.values
    .filter { !it.completed }
    .onEach { println("Processing task ${it.id}") }
    .map { it.description.uppercase() }
    .forEach(::println)
```

The **onEach** logs each task ID before mapping its description. Because it returns the same list, mapping proceeds uninterrupted. This pattern keeps logging or metrics close to the data flow without separate loops.

Combining Multiple Pipelines

You can define several pipelines and then merge their results. For example, to produce a combined report of overdue and upcoming tasks:

```
val now = System.currentTimeMillis()
val overdue = tasks.values
    .filter { !it.completed && it.dueTimestamp < now }
    .sortedBy { it.dueTimestamp }
    .map { "OVERDUE: ${it.id} due
${formatTime(it.dueTimestamp)}" }
val upcoming = tasks.values
    .filter { !it.completed && it.dueTimestamp in now until
now + DAY_MS }
    .sortedBy { it.dueTimestamp }
    .map { "UPCOMING: ${it.id} due
${formatTime(it.dueTimestamp)}" }
```

```
(val overdue + upcoming).forEach(::println)
```

By separating pipelines for different categories and then concatenating their results, we create a unified report without tangled loops or interleaved logic.

Parallelizing Pipelines Safely

The function chaining lends itself to parallel execution when we need performance. By converting a collection to a Kotlin sequence—**`asSequence()`**—you defer evaluation and avoid intermediate allocations until we call a terminal operation (**`toList()`**, **`forEach`**). For large task sets, we write:

```
tasks.values.asSequence()
    .filter { !it.completed }
    .map { transformTask(it) }
    .sortedBy { it.createdTimestamp }
    .toList()
    .forEach(::println)
```

The pipeline runs lazily, applying each transformation only as needed, which can offer efficiency gains in long chains.

Safe Composition with Null-Aware Functions

When some lambdas may return **`null`**, we can compose with **`mapNotNull`** to filter and transform in one step:

```
tasks.values
    .mapNotNull { task ->
        if (task.description.contains("!"))
task.description.removePrefix("!") else null
    }
    .forEach { println("Cleaned: $it") }
```

This pattern applies a mapping that might drop elements, then processes only the non-null results, preventing **`null`** values from propagating.

This approach turns our app into a functional powerhouse, where each stage in the chain focuses on a single responsibility, and the overall behavior reads like a natural sequence of data manipulations.

Optimizing Event Handling

So far, we have built an observer pattern with concrete **TaskObserver** implementations, but each new listener required a separate class or object. Lambdas let us replace that boilerplate with inline callbacks, binding event logic directly at the registration point. By supplying anonymous functions for **onTaskAdded**, **onTaskUpdated**, and **onTaskRemoved**, we keep our event-handling code close to where the service is configured, improving readability and maintainability. The lambdas also integrate seamlessly with coroutine-based flows, channels, and callbacks, enabling asynchronous reactions to state changes without introducing additional classes or cluttering our codebase.

Registering Lambda-Based Observers

Rather than implementing **TaskObserver** manually, we define a helper extension on **TaskService** that accepts lambdas for each event:

```
fun TaskService.onTaskEvents(
    added: (Task) -> Unit = {},
    updated: (Task) -> Unit = {},
    removed: (Int) -> Unit = {}
) {
    addObserver(object : TaskObserver {
        override fun onTaskAdded(task: Task)   = added(task)
        override fun onTaskUpdated(task: Task) = updated(task)
        override fun onTaskRemoved(id: Int)    = removed(id)
    })
}
```

At startup, we attach inline handlers:

```
service.onTaskEvents(
    added   = { println("▶️ Task ${it.id} added:
${it.description}") },
    updated = { println("➕ Task ${it.id} updated:
completed=${it.completed}") },
    removed = { println("✖️ Task $it removed") }
```

```
)
```

This registration replaces three separate classes with a single lambda-based call. We see immediately which actions correspond to each event, without scrolling through unrelated code.

Asynchronous Updates with Lambdas and Flows

For real-time UIs or background processing, we can expose a **`StateFlow`** of events from **`TaskService`**. Inside **`TaskService`**, define:

```
private val _events = MutableSharedFlow<TaskEvent>()
val events: SharedFlow<TaskEvent> = _events
sealed class TaskEvent {
  data class Added(val task: Task): TaskEvent()
  data class Updated(val task: Task): TaskEvent()
  data class Removed(val id: Int): TaskEvent()
}
```

Then we emit events in mutation methods:

```
suspend fun addTask(task: Task): Int {
    tasks[task.id] = task; save()
    _events.emit(TaskEvent.Added(task))
    return task.id
}
```

Next, in our main coroutine context, collect events with lambdas:

```
GlobalScope.launch {
    service.events.collect { event ->
        when (event) {
            is TaskEvent.Added   -> println("📥 [Flow] Added
${event.task.id}")
            is TaskEvent.Updated -> println("🔄 [Flow] Updated
${event.task.id}")
```

```
            is TaskEvent.Removed -> println("🗑 [Flow] Removed
${event.id}")
        }
    }
}
```

By passing a lambda to **collect**, we handle events asynchronously as they arrive, decoupled from the REPL loop. Our application remains responsive because event handling occurs in its own coroutine.

Integrating Lambdas in Reminder System

Previously, we polled overdue tasks in a loop. Now we react to additions and completions via lambdas and channels. Use our **onTaskEvents** helper alongside a **Channel<Task>**:

```
val reminderChannel = Channel<Task>(Channel.BUFFERED)
service.onTaskEvents(
    added   = { if (!it.completed) reminderChannel.offer(it)
},
    updated = { if (it.completed) reminderChannel.removeIf {
task -> task.id == it.id } }
)
GlobalScope.launch {
    for (task in reminderChannel) {
        delay(60_000)
        println("⏰ Reminder: Task ${task.id} is still
pending.")
    }
}
```

You inline both the event logic—filtering added tasks and removing completed ones—and the asynchronous processing in a coroutine. Lambdas keep the code concise, and channels ensure backpressure and ordered delivery.

Composing Event-Driven Pipelines

The combine of **SharedFlow** and functional operators helps us to create pipelines that transform events before handling:

```
GlobalScope.launch {
    service.events
        .filterIsInstance<TaskEvent.Added>()
        .map { it.task }
        .filter { it.highPriority }
        .collect { println(" Priority task added: ${it.id}")
}
}
```

In the above, we filter only **Added** events, extract the **Task**, then filter for **highPriority**. Each stage uses inline lambdas (**filterIsInstance**, **map**, **filter**), building a reactive pipeline that responds only to the events we care about.

Summary

To sum up, we explored how lambda expressions serve as concise, anonymous functions in Kotlin, defining them with **{ parameters -> body }** syntax and using the implicit **it** for single-parameter cases. We learned how inline functions eliminate lambda-object allocations by copying bodies at call sites, ensuring high-performance callbacks.

We then applied lambdas to collection operations—chaining **filter**, **map**, and **fold** calls—to select incomplete, high-priority tasks, transform them into summary strings or JSON lines, and aggregate estimated durations without manual loops or temporary lists. We discovered **flatMap** for flattening nested tag lists, **onEach** for injecting side-effects such as logging within pipelines, and lazy sequences via **asSequence()** for efficient, on-demand evaluation.

Finally, we streamlined event handling by defining a **onTaskEvents** helper that accepts lambdas for added, updated, and removed callbacks, replacing boilerplate observer classes. We integrated coroutines with **SharedFlow** and channels, using lambdas in **collect**, **filterIsInstance**, and **map** operators to build reactive pipelines for logging, reminders, and audit trails.

Chapter 9: Error Handling and Type Casting

Chapter Overview

This chapter starts teaching us to enclose code that might throw exceptions within **try-catch** blocks, catching specific types such as **NumberFormatException** and **IOException** to provide immediate feedback and avoid crashes. We will explore using **try** as an expression to return fallback values and **finally** blocks to guarantee resource cleanup, ensuring that file streams and connections close reliably. Next, we will apply safe cast operators (**as?**) when processing dynamic data—metadata maps or manual JSON parsing—to prevent **ClassCastException** and handle invalid types elegantly.

After that, we will implement a centralized logging component—**ErrorLogger**—to record errors uniformly with timestamps, context, and stack traces, replacing ad-hoc prints with a single file-based log. We will then create a higher-order **safeExecute** function that wraps risky operations, automatically logs exceptions, and returns safe defaults, refactoring our load, save, and dispatch logic to use it for robust recovery. Finally, we will integrate our error-handling framework with observers and optional remote reporting—emitting error events to listeners and sending telemetry—so that our app maintains control flow, assists the user when things go wrong, and supplies developers with clear diagnostics for troubleshooting.

Exception Management with 'Try-Catch'

We have heard so far that the developers encounter unforeseen errors: invalid input, missing files, serialization failures, or unexpected null references. Without proper handling, our application crashes, leaving users frustrated and data at risk. The Kotlin's **try-catch** blocks let us intercept exceptions at runtime, respond gracefully, and maintain control flow. By wrapping risky operations in **try** blocks and catching specific exceptions, we ensure that even when something goes wrong, our app can log the error, notify the user, and continue operating. So here, we will look towards to use **try-catch** as both a statement and an expression, implement cleanup logic with **finally**, and apply these patterns in our app to improve reliability and user experience during unforeseen events.

'try-catch' Syntax and Flow

A **try** block encloses code that may throw. Following it, one or more **catch** clauses specify exception types to handle. Optionally, a **finally** block runs whether or not an exception occurred as below:

```
try {
    // risky operation
} catch (e: SpecificException) {
```

```
    // handle known issue
} catch (e: Exception) {
    // fallback for other errors
} finally {
    // cleanup actions
}
```

Kotlin also treats **try** as an expression returning a value, enabling we to assign its result directly:

```
val result = try {
    parseInput(input)
} catch (e: NumberFormatException) {
    println("Invalid number.")
    null
}
```

In the above, the **result** is either the parsed value or **null** if parsing failed.

Handling User Input Safely

You parse task IDs from user commands, turning strings into integers. Without guards, invalid input crashes the app:

```
val id: Int = input.removePrefix("remove ").toInt()  // throws
on non-numeric
```

Wrap parsing in **try-catch** to catch **NumberFormatException**:

```
val id = try {
    input.removePrefix("remove ").toInt()
} catch (e: NumberFormatException) {
    println("Please enter a numeric ID.")
    return
}
handleRemove(id)
```

By returning early when parsing fails, we prevent downstream errors and keep the REPL loop alive.

Protecting File I/O and JSON Serialization

When saving and loading tasks via JSON, we depend on file system and serialization libraries. Errors such as **`IOException`** or **`SerializationException`** can occur. We encapsulate file operations in a **`try-catch`** block:

```
fun loadTasks(): Map<Int, Task> {
    return try {
        val text = File("tasks.json").readText()
        json.decodeFromString(text)
    } catch (e: FileNotFoundException) {
        println("No existing data found; starting fresh.")
        emptyMap()
    } catch (e: SerializationException) {
        println("Data corrupted; resetting tasks.")
        emptyMap()
    }
}
```

When writing:

```
fun saveTasks(tasks: Map<Int, Task>) {
    try {
        val text = json.encodeToString(tasks)
        File("tasks.json").writeText(text)
    } catch (e: IOException) {
        println("Failed to save tasks: ${e.message}")
    }
}
```

This ensures that disk errors or format issues do not crash the application, and users understand what happened.

Using 'finally' for Resource Cleanup

When working with resources like file streams or database connections, we need to close them regardless of success or failure. So here, we often use **use** for auto-closing, but for demonstrations:

```
val reader = File("config.txt").bufferedReader()
try {
    val settings = reader.readText()
    // parse settings
} catch (e: IOException) {
    println("Error reading configuration.")
} finally {
    reader.close()
}
```

In the above, the **finally** guarantees that **reader.close()** executes, preventing resource leaks even if an exception interrupted **readText()**.

Catching Multiple Exception Types

When a **try** block may throw different exceptions, catch them separately to provide tailored responses:

```
try {
    val id = args.toInt()
    val task = service.getTask(id) ?: throw
NoSuchElementException("ID not found")
    markComplete(task)
} catch (e: NumberFormatException) {
    println("Enter a valid task ID.")
} catch (e: NoSuchElementException) {
    println(e.message)
}
```

This pattern distinguishes between parsing errors and business-logic errors, enhancing UX with precise feedback.

By systematically applying **try-catch** blocks around parsing, I/O, and high-level dispatch, we dramatically improved our app's resilience, ensuring that unforeseen events do not interrupt the user's workflow.

Utilizing Safe Cast Operators

There are a few things you often work with that have values whose types aren't guaranteed at compile time. Some examples are JSON payloads parsed into **Any?**, dynamic plugin data, or user-supplied maps of settings. The regular cast operator (**as**) on an incompatible type triggers a **ClassCastException** and crashes our app. Kotlin's safe cast operator (**as?**) prevents this by attempting the cast and returning **null** on failure instead of throwing.

For example, if we have a mixed map of properties—**val props: Map<String, Any?>**—and we expect a list of tags under **"tags"**, we cast safely:

```
val raw = props["tags"]
val tags: List<String>? = raw as? List<String>
```

If **raw** isn't a **List<String>**, **tags** becomes **null**, and we can handle that case gracefully—no exception. We wrap the result in an **if** or an Elvis fallback:

```
val safeTags = tags ?: emptyList()
```

This pattern ensures that our app continues operating even when external data doesn't match expectations.

Applying Safe Casts to User Input Parsing

In our REPL loop, we parse commands into any-typed parameters or read dynamic configuration values. Suppose we allow users to supply custom metadata as key-value pairs in a map of **Map<String, Any?>**.

When handling a **"setPriority"** command, we fetch the priority value and safe-cast it to an integer:

```
fun handleSetPriority(args: String, metadata: Map<String,
Any?>) {
    val key = args.trim()
    val rawValue = metadata[key]
    val priority: Int = (rawValue as? Int) ?: run {
```

```
        println("Priority for $key must be a number.")
        return
    }
    // proceed with a valid Int priority
    service.setPriority(key, priority)
    println("Priority of $key set to $priority")
}
```

In the above, the **rawValue as? Int** avoids a **ClassCastException** if the user supplied a string or boolean by mistake. By checking for **null**, we detect invalid types, inform the user, and exit the handler.

Safe Casting in Collection and JSON

When loading tasks from a JSON file without a serializer—say, manually parsing a nested **Map<String, Any?>**—you need to extract fields safely. Consider a fragment of deserialization:

```
fun parseTask(data: Map<String, Any?>): Task? {
    val id = (data["id"] as? Double)?.toInt() ?: return null
    val desc = data["description"] as? String ?: return null
    val high = data["highPriority"] as? Boolean ?: false
    val completed = data["completed"] as? Boolean ?: false
    val timestamp = (data["createdTimestamp"] as?
Double)?.toLong() ?: System.currentTimeMillis()
    return Task(id, desc, highPriority = high, completed =
completed, createdTimestamp = timestamp)
}
```

By chaining safe casts and Elvis fallbacks, we convert loosely-typed JSON values into our **Task** data class. Numeric JSON values often arrive as **Double** from a generic parser, so we cast to **Double**, then convert to **Int** or **Long**. If any required field is missing or of the wrong type, we bail out safely—returning **null** and skipping that entry rather than crashing.

Centralized Error Logging and Recovery

You'll run into different kinds of errors while building the Task Tracker. There are a few things that can cause parsing errors. It can happen when user input doesn't match the expected formats. So, for example, if the user enters a non-numeric ID or malformed command. You'll get I/O errors when you're reading or writing the JSON file. These could be due to missing permissions, a disk full error, or broken paths. If the JSON structure changes without warning or fields vanish, you'll run into serialization errors. Errors that happen when different coroutines access shared state without coordinating can be called concurrency errors. And finally, there are unexpected runtime exceptions—null pointers, index out of bounds, or arithmetic failures—that can interrupt program flow. If we catalog these categories from the start, we can handle each one with the right logging, recovery strategies, and clear user feedback. That way we can avoid letting the app crash unpredictably.

Designing Central Error Logger

Instead of scattering **println** statements or ad-hoc file writes across the codebase, we create a single **ErrorLogger** to capture all exceptions consistently.

To do this, we then definethe following in **ErrorLogger.kt**:

```
object ErrorLogger {
    private val logFile = File("error.log")
    fun log(e: Throwable, context: String = "") {
        val timestamp = DateTimeFormatter.ISO_INSTANT
            .format(Instant.now())
        val entry = buildString {
            append("$timestamp ERROR")
            if (context.isNotBlank()) append(" in $context")
            append(": ${e::class.simpleName} -
${e.message}\n")
            e.stackTrace.take(5).forEach {
                append("\tat $it\n")
            }
        }
        logFile.appendText(entry)
    }
}
```

Here, you use a timestamped, one-entry-per-exception format that includes a brief stack trace. By centralizing logging, we ensure uniform log entries and one file to inspect—making debugging more efficient.

Wrapping Risky Operations

You leverage a higher-order function to wrap any code block that may throw, automatically logging and recovering. In **TaskService.kt**, add:

```
inline fun <T> safeExecute(context: String, block: () -> T):
T? {
    return try {
        block()
    } catch (e: Throwable) {
        ErrorLogger.log(e, context)
        null
    }
}
```

You then refactor methods to use **safeExecute**:

```
fun loadTasks(): Map<Int, Task> = safeExecute("loadTasks") {
    val text = File("tasks.json").readText()
    json.decodeFromString(text)
} ?: emptyMap()
fun saveTasks(tasks: Map<Int, Task>) {
    safeExecute("saveTasks") {
        val text = json.encodeToString(tasks)
        File("tasks.json").writeText(text)
    }
}
```

With wrapping the core logic, we catch any exception, log it, and return a safe fallback (**null** or **Unit**). This pattern scales to parsing, network calls, or any module we add later.

Integrating with Command Dispatch

You also guard the top-level dispatch loop to log unexpected errors without exposing stack traces to the user:

```
while (true) {
    print("> ")
    val input = readLine().orEmpty().trim()
    safeExecute("dispatchCommand") {
        dispatchCommand(input)
    }
}
```

If **dispatchCommand** throws due to a bug, **safeExecute** logs the error context and returns **null**, letting the loop continue. Users see no crash, and we have a record of what went wrong.

Recovery Strategies

The logging alone isn't enough, we want the Task Tracker to recover gracefully. For parsing IDs:

```
val id = safeExecute("parseId") {
    args.toInt()
} ?: run {
    println("Invalid ID format. Please enter a number.")
    return
}
```

In the above, if parsing fails, **safeExecute** logs the **NumberFormatException**, and we handle the **null** return by prompting the user. For file I/O, we can retry once before giving up:

```
fun saveWithRetry(tasks: Map<Int, Task>) {
    repeat(2) { attempt ->
        if (safeExecute("saveTasks attempt ${attempt+1}") {

File("tasks.json").writeText(json.encodeToString(tasks))
```

```
            } != null) return
        Thread.sleep(500)
    }
    println("Failed to save tasks after retries. Check
error.log.")
}
```

From above, if we combinelogging with retries and user messages, we can deliver a more resilient application.

Alerting Observers on Fatal Errors

For severe failures—such as database corruption or unrecoverable state—you inform all parts of the application via an error event. To do this, within **TaskService**, we can extend our observer pattern with an error callback:

```
interface TaskObserver {
    fun onError(e: Throwable, context: String)
    // existing methods…
}
fun addObserver(observer: TaskObserver) { /*…*/ }
```

When **safeExecute** catches an exception, we notify observers:

```
catch (e: Throwable) {
    ErrorLogger.log(e, context)
    observers.forEach { it.onError(e, context) }
    return null
}
```

A **UIObserver** can then display an alert to the user:

```
class UIObserver: TaskObserver {
    override fun onError(e: Throwable, context: String) {
        println("An error occurred in $context. Please retry
or contact support.")
```

```
    }
    // ...
}
```

This immediate feedback helps users understand when operations fail and prevents silent data loss.

Harmonizing Logs with Monitoring Tools

If we integrate with external monitoring—such as sending logs to a remote server—you adapt **ErrorLogger.log** to include an HTTP POST:

```
fun log(e: Throwable, context: String = "") {
    // existing file append
    try {
        HttpClient.post("https://monitor.gitforgits.com/log")
{
            body = mapOf("timestamp" to timestamp, "context"
to context, "error" to e.toString())
        }
    } catch (_: Exception) { /* ignore network failures */ }
}
```

By centralizing this logic, we ensure consistent telemetry without sprinkling network calls across our code. Through systematic categorization of error types, a centralized logger, safe-execution wrappers, recovery strategies, observer notifications, and optional remote reporting, we build a Task Tracker that provides clear diagnostics and user guidance, thereby transforming errors from crashes into manageable incidents.

Summary

To sum up, we learned to wrap the risky operations in **try-catch** blocks to intercept exceptions including parsing errors, I/O failures, and serialization issues. We then used **try** as an expression to return fallback values when parsing IDs or loading JSON, and we applied **finally** to close resources reliably. We adopted safe casts (**as?**) when converting loosely typed data—metadata maps or generic JSON objects—so that invalid types yielded **null** instead of **ClassCastException**, letting we handle unexpected values gracefully. We introduced a centralized **ErrorLogger** singleton to record timestamps, exception details, and stack traces to a log file, replacing scattered **println** statements with a uniform logging mechanism.

We created a higher-order **safeExecute** wrapper that logged any thrown exception and returned safe defaults, then refactored file I/O and command dispatch to use it, preserving control flow and user experience during failures. We implemented recovery strategies—such as retry loops for save operations—and extended our observer pattern to notify listeners of fatal errors, driving UI alerts and background responses. We even sketched remote telemetry by posting error data to a monitoring endpoint, all through centralized logic. These practices transformed uncaught exceptions into managed incidents, bolstered application resilience, and provided clear diagnostics for debugging without interrupting the user's workflow.

Chapter 10: Handling JSON and Data Serialization

Chapter Overview

In this new chapter, we begin with exploring to parse JSON strings into Kotlin objects using **`kotlinx.serialization`**, annotating our **`Task`** class with **`@Serializable`** and configuring **`Json`** to ignore unknown keys so that evolving schemas do not break our parser.

Next, we will reverse the process by serializing **`Task`** instances back into JSON text with **`encodeToString`**, exploring both compact and pretty-printed formats and centralizing file writes in our service layer for consistent persistence. After that, we will compare alternative libraries—Moshi and Jackson Kotlin module—integrating each into our build, generating adapters, and benchmarking their performance to determine which offers the best throughput for our app's needs. Then, we will tackle nested JSON structures by defining layered DTO classes with **`@SerialName`** mappings, parsing hierarchical API responses into **`TaskResponse`**, **`Meta`**, and **`TaskDto`** objects, and mapping those DTOs into our domain **`Task`** entities.

Finally, we will handle dynamic or deeply nested fields with **`JsonObject`**, and write custom serializers for special types such as ISO-format timestamps, ensuring that every element in complex JSON payloads maps accurately into our application model before validation and business-logic integration.

Parsing JSON

There are a few things that you'll need to do with data interchange. First, you'll need to connect our app with external services. You'll also need to use it to persist state between sessions and integrate with other tools. JavaScript Object Notation—or JSON—is now the go-to for web APIs, configuration files, and lightweight data storage. Its human-readable text format, support across languages, and simple object and array structure make JSON great for sending task lists to a mobile client or reading user preferences at startup. When we correctly parse JSON into Kotlin objects, we gain type safety and eliminate the need for manual string manipulation. Instead of splitting on braces or indexing quotes, we let a JSON library handle escape sequences, nested structures, and missing fields. When you convert raw JSON into domain classes—like our **`Task`** data class—you focus on business logic instead of error-prone parsing code. It's great for handling JSON, and when our app reads a file or gets API responses, it turns strings into fully formed **`Task`** instances with minimal boilerplate, robust error checking, and consistent behavior whenever the JSON schema changes.

JSON Strings into Objects

We can utilize the Kotlin's official serialization library—kotlinx.serialization—to parse JSON into objects with concise annotations and extension functions. To do this, in our Gradle setup, we add the plugin and dependency:

```
plugins {
    kotlin("plugin.serialization") version "2.0.20"
}
dependencies {
    implementation("org.jetbrains.kotlinx:kotlinx-
serialization-json:1.6.0")
}
```

Next, annotate our **Task** class in **Task.kt**:

```
import kotlinx.serialization.Serializable
@Serializable
data class Task(
    val id: Int,
    val description: String,
    val highPriority: Boolean = false,
    val completed: Boolean = false,
    val createdTimestamp: Long
)
```

To parse a JSON string into a list of tasks, we call:

```
import kotlinx.serialization.decodeFromString
import kotlinx.serialization.json.Json
fun parseTasks(jsonString: String): List<Task> {
    return Json { ignoreUnknownKeys = true }
        .decodeFromString(jsonString)
}
```

In the above, the **ignoreUnknownKeys = true** lets us evolve our JSON structure without breaking parsing when extra fields appear. By wrapping this logic in a dedicated function, we centralize error handling and schema management. In our **TaskService**, we integrate parsing during startup:

```kotlin
val initialTasks = try {
    val text = File("tasks.json").readText()
    parseTasks(text)
} catch (e: Exception) {
    println("Failed to load tasks: ${e.message}")
    emptyList()
}
initialTasks.forEach { addTask(it) }
```

This strategy transforms raw JSON into typed **Task** objects immediately, ensuring that the rest of our application operates on structured, validated instances rather than raw strings or untyped maps.

Serializing Kotlin Objects into JSON Format

Encoding Objects with 'kotlinx.serialization'

You already transformed JSON text into **Task** instances; now we reverse the flow, converting in-memory **Task** objects back into JSON for persistence or API communication. With kotlinx.serialization, we avoid manual string concatenation and ensure that our JSON output matches our data model automatically. In **Task.kt**, we have the **@Serializable** annotation on our **Task** data class. To serialize a single task or an entire collection, invoke the extension function **encodeToString**.

For example, to convert a list of tasks into a compact JSON array, we write:

```kotlin
import kotlinx.serialization.encodeToString
import kotlinx.serialization.json.Json
fun serializeTasks(tasks: List<Task>): String {
    return Json { ignoreUnknownKeys = true }
        .encodeToString(tasks)
}
```

You passed our task list directly to **encodeToString**, and the library produced a JSON string representing each object's properties—ID, description, priority, completion flag, and timestamp.

If we prefer a more human-readable format when inspecting files, enable pretty printing:

```
fun serializeTasksPretty(tasks: List<Task>): String {
    return Json {
        prettyPrint = true
        prettyPrintIndent = "  "
        encodeDefaults = true
    }.encodeToString(tasks)
}
```

By specifying **prettyPrint**, we instruct the serializer to insert line breaks and indentation, making our **tasks.json** file legible in editors. The **encodeDefaults** flag ensures that properties with default values—such as **completed = false**—also appear in the output, which can be helpful for clients that expect explicit fields.

Writing JSON to Disk and External Endpoints

After producing the JSON string, we commonly write it to a file or send it over HTTP using the Kotlin's **java.io.File** APIs:

```
fun saveTasksToFile(tasks: List<Task>, path: String = "tasks.json") {
    val jsonString = serializeTasksPretty(tasks)
    File(path).writeText(jsonString)
}
```

This function replaces any existing file content with fresh JSON, guaranteeing that our persistent store always reflects the current in-memory state. To integrate this into our **TaskService**, replace the manual serialization and file-writing code with a single call to **saveTasksToFile** inside our save logic:

```
fun saveTasks() {
    safeExecute("saveTasks") {
        saveTasksToFile(tasks.values.toList())
    }
}
```

By funneling all serialization through **serializeTasksPretty**, we maintain a single point of configuration for JSON formatting. If we later switch to a remote storage endpoint, we can adapt **saveTasksToFile** to perform an HTTP POST instead of a file write, without changing the core serialization code.

Integrating Default and Custom Serializers

When our **Task** class grows—for example, adding an enum for priority levels or a **LocalDate** due date—you customize serialization with contextual serializers. In our module setup, register serializers in the **Json** builder:

```
val customJson = Json {
    serializersModule = SerializersModule {
        contextual(LocalDate::class, LocalDateSerializer)
    }
    ignoreUnknownKeys = true
}
```

Then call **customJson.encodeToString(tasks)** to handle those new types automatically. This modular approach keeps our serialization logic robust as our data model evolves.

Using Serialization Libraries

You already saw how kotlinx.serialization offers first-class support in Kotlin projects, but the ecosystem includes other mature libraries—Moshi and Jackson Kotlin module—that excel in specific scenarios. Moshi provides a straightforward API with annotation-driven adapters, while Jackson's Kotlin module delivers powerful schema evolution, streaming, and polymorphic handling. By understanding the strengths of each, we can pick the most efficient tool for our app's JSON workloads—whether we need zero-reflection runtime performance, extensive configuration options, or seamless interoperability with Java code.

Integrating Moshi

To add Moshi, we first include the Gradle dependency and codegen plugin:

```
plugins {
    kotlin("kapt") version "2.0.20"
}
dependencies {
```

```
    implementation("com.squareup.moshi:moshi:1.15.0")
    kapt("com.squareup.moshi:moshi-kotlin-codegen:1.15.0")
}
```

Then we annotate our **Task** class for Moshi code generation:

```
import com.squareup.moshi.JsonClass
@JsonClass(generateAdapter = true)
data class Task(
    val id: Int,
    val description: String,
    val highPriority: Boolean = false,
    val completed: Boolean = false,
    val createdTimestamp: Long
)
```

After this, we initialize a **Moshi** instance with the Kotlin adapter factory:

```
val moshi = Moshi.Builder()
    .add(KotlinJsonAdapterFactory())
    .build()
val taskAdapter =
moshi.adapter<List<Task>>(Types.newParameterizedType(List::cla
ss.java, Task::class.java))
```

You can then parse and serialize efficiently:

```
// Parsing
val tasks: List<Task> =
taskAdapter.fromJson(jsonString).orEmpty()
// Serializing
val jsonOutput: String = taskAdapter.toJson(taskList)
```

Because Moshi's code-generated adapters avoid reflection, these operations run with minimal overhead—ideal when our app loads or saves large task collections.

Configuring Jackson with Kotlin Module

When we require advanced features—such as polymorphic types for different **Command** subclasses or streaming large data sets—Jackson's Kotlin module shines. Add dependencies:

```
dependencies {
    implementation("com.fasterxml.jackson.module:jackson-module-kotlin:2.15.2")
    implementation("com.fasterxml.jackson.core:jackson-databind:2.15.2")
}
```

We then register the module in our mapper setup:

```
val mapper = jacksonObjectMapper()
    .registerKotlinModule()

.configure(DeserializationFeature.FAIL_ON_UNKNOWN_PROPERTIES, false)
```

To parse JSON into tasks:

```
val tasks: List<Task> = mapper.readValue(jsonString)
```

And then to write out our in-memory state:

```
val jsonOutput: String =
mapper.writerWithDefaultPrettyPrinter()
    .writeValueAsString(taskList)
```

The Jackson supports incremental parsing via **JsonParser** for streaming large arrays without loading everything into memory, and its polymorphic annotations let us handle subclasses of **Command** or **TaskEvent** seamlessly.

Selecting and Benchmarking Serializer

With multiple options in place, we measure performance to decide our choice. The Kotlin's **measureTimeMillis** helps to compare serialization and deserialization speeds:

```
val repetitions = 100
```

```
val sampleJson = serializeTasksPretty(tasks)
val kotlinxTime = measureTimeMillis {
    repeat(repetitions) {
Json.decodeFromString<List<Task>>(sampleJson) }
}
val moshiTime = measureTimeMillis {
    repeat(repetitions) { taskAdapter.fromJson(sampleJson) }
}
val jacksonTime = measureTimeMillis {
    repeat(repetitions) {
mapper.readValue<List<Task>>(sampleJson) }
}
println("kotlinx: $kotlinxTime ms, moshi: $moshiTime ms,
jackson: $jacksonTime ms")
```

When we run these benchmarks on our Linux environment, we can see which library offers the best throughput for our typical task payload size. This lets us optimize for startup speed, memory footprint, or developer productivity.

Overall, we centralize configuration in our service layer, allowing we to switch serializers later with minimal code changes, and we gain confidence that our app can handle evolving schemas and performance demands gracefully.

Managing Complex JSON Structures

A lot of APIs give you more than just simple arrays of tasks. You often get rich, hierarchical payloads that include metadata, data arrays, embedded objects with user details, and nested lists of comments or tags within each task. If you want to handle these complex structures robustly, you've got to map every level of the JSON hierarchy into Kotlin's type system. That way, your code will work with fully typed objects rather than raw **`JsonObjects`**. We make sure that each JSON field—no matter how deeply nested—lands in the correct property, complete with type safety and null handling, by defining nested data classes, using annotations like **`@SerialName`**, and employing custom serializers when needed. This method gives you some pretty powerful IDE support, compile-time schema checks, and seamless navigation of multi-level data in our app.

Defining Nested Data Classes

Now suppose the API returns a response like this:

```json
{
  "status": "ok",
  "meta": {
    "page": 1,
    "pageSize": 20,
    "totalCount": 57
  },
  "tasks": [
    {
      "id": 42,
      "description": "Review PR",
      "high_priority": true,
      "completed": false,
      "created_timestamp": 1672531200000,
      "tags": ["code", "review"],
      "assignee": {
        "userId": 7,
        "userName": "alice"
      }
    }
  ]
}
```

You model this with nested **`@Serializable`** classes:

```kotlin
@Serializable
data class TaskResponse(
    val status: String,
    val meta: Meta,
    val tasks: List<TaskDto>
```

```
)
@Serializable
data class Meta(
    val page: Int,
    val pageSize: Int,
    val totalCount: Int
)
@Serializable
data class TaskDto(
    val id: Int,
    val description: String,
    @SerialName("high_priority") val highPriority: Boolean =
false,
    val completed: Boolean = false,
    @SerialName("created_timestamp") val createdTimestamp:
Long,
    val tags: List<String> = emptyList(),
    val assignee: Assignee
)
@Serializable
data class Assignee(
    val userId: Int,
    val userName: String
)
```

Here, the annotations like **`@SerialName("high_priority")`** map snake_case JSON keys to camelCase Kotlin properties. Default values (**`= false`**, **`= emptyList()`**) handle missing fields gracefully.

Parsing Nested Structure into Domain Models

After decoding into DTOs, we convert them into our domain **`Task`** class. In **`TaskService`**, write:

```
fun loadFromApi(jsonString: String): List<Task> {
    val response = Json { ignoreUnknownKeys = true }
        .decodeFromString<TaskResponse>(jsonString)
    return response.tasks.map { dto ->
        Task(
            id = dto.id,
            description = dto.description,
            highPriority = dto.highPriority,
            completed = dto.completed,
            createdTimestamp = dto.createdTimestamp
        ).also { task ->
            // attach tags or metadata as needed
            dto.tags.forEach { tag -> service.addTag(task.id,
tag) }
            val assignee = dto.assignee
            println("Task ${task.id} assigned to
${assignee.userName}")
        }
    }
}
```

This two-stage process—decode into DTO classes, then map to domain entities—keeps JSON concerns isolated from core business logic.

Handling Dynamic Structures

When JSON contains arbitrary key sets or dynamic sub-objects, we can use **`JsonElement`** and **`JsonObject`** for parts of the payload. For example, if each task can have custom fields under **`"attributes"`**, write:

```
@Serializable
data class TaskDto(
    /* … previous fields … */,
```

```
    val attributes: JsonObject = JsonObject(emptyMap())
)
```

Then, after parsing:

```
val priorityLevel =
taskDto.attributes["priorityLevel"]?.jsonPrimitive?.intOrNull
?: 0
```

This gives us direct access to nested JSON without needing to predefine every possible field.

Custom Serializers

Sometimes date formats or enum values require custom handling. If **`created_timestamp`** was an ISO string instead of epoch milliseconds, we create a **`@Serializer`** object:

```
object InstantSerializer : KSerializer<Instant> {
    override val descriptor =
PrimitiveSerialDescriptor("Instant", PrimitiveKind.STRING)
    override fun deserialize(decoder: Decoder) =
        Instant.parse(decoder.decodeString())
    override fun serialize(encoder: Encoder, value: Instant) =
        encoder.encodeString(value.toString())
}
```

Then apply it in our DTO:

```
@Serializable
data class TaskDto(
    /* … */,
    @Serializable(with = InstantSerializer::class)
    @SerialName("created_timestamp")
    val created: Instant
)
```

Our code now parses ISO timestamps into **`Instant`** objects automatically, simplifying downstream date computations.

Validating Nested Data at Runtime

When we need to enforce business rules—such as ensuring every task has at least one tag—you add checks after parsing:

```
response.tasks.forEach { dto ->
    require(dto.tags.isNotEmpty()) { "Task ${dto.id} must have at least one tag." }
}
```

If we fail fast on invalid data, we can prevent inconsistent data from spreading through our application. This kind of robust modeling makes sure our app can handle complex stuff, like pagination, metadata, user objects, and dynamic attributes. This lets us focus on the main logic instead of on weak parsing code.

Summary

Just to summarize the learnings, we very well transformed raw JSON text into strongly typed **`Task`** objects by annotating our data classes with **`@Serializable`** and using kotlinx.serialization's **`decodeFromString`**, handling unknown keys and fallback values gracefully. We reversed the flow with **`encodeToString`**, configuring **`Json`** for pretty printing and default inclusion, then centralized file writes in our service for consistent output. We explored alternative libraries—Moshi for reflection-free adapters and Jackson Kotlin module for polymorphic and streaming support—measuring their performance via **`measureTimeMillis`** to choose the best fit for our payload sizes.

We then modeled nested API responses with layered DTO classes—**`TaskResponse`**, **`Meta`**, **`TaskDto`**, and **`Assignee`**—using **`@SerialName`** to map snake_case JSON to camelCase properties, and we mapped DTOs into our domain **`Task`** entities, isolating parsing concerns. We handled dynamic or deeply nested fields with **`JsonObject`** and **`JsonElement`**, safely extracting values without predetermined schema. For special cases like ISO timestamp strings or custom enum formats, we wrote custom **`KSerializer`** implementations and registered them contextually to convert JSON fields into **`Instant`** or other types. We defined precise serializers, used default parameters, and validated data post-parsing. This ensured seamless integration of complex JSON structures from APIs or files into our app's in-memory model, paving the way for robust communication and persistent storage.

CHAPTER 11: DESIGNING RESTFUL APIs

Chapter Overview

In this chapter, we're going to start by looking at REST principles—like resource orientation, statelessness, and standard URI design—to model our app's entities as HTTP resources under a versioned path. Then, we'll check out how to apply all this in Ktor's routing DSL, making sure we safely extract path and query parameters, and decode JSON request bodies into DTOs for creation and updates. Next, we'll integrate persistent storage by defining database schemas with Exposed, mapping entities to our domain **`Task`** class, and wiring repository methods into our API endpoints so that tasks survive restarts. Finally, we'll use JWT-based authentication, TLS encryption, input validation, rate limiting, CORS/CSRF protections, and comprehensive request logging to secure our API.

RESTful API Overview

The APIs we design show off what our app can do—like adding tasks, listing them, and marking them as complete—to outside clients, like web dashboards or mobile apps. Basically, REST is an architectural style that focuses on resources identified by URIs. Each task in our system becomes a resource at a unique path, for example **`/tasks/42`**. By thinking in terms of resources rather than RPC-style commands, we create an intuitive, discoverable interface. Clients make HTTP requests—**`GET`**, **`POST`**, **`PUT`**, **`DELETE`**—to interact with these resources. REST encourages statelessness: each request from the client must contain all information needed to process it. Because the server does not retain session state, our app endpoints scale more easily, and intermediaries like load balancers can distribute requests without sticky sessions. We will model our tasks, task lists, and related entities (such as tags or users) as resources with clear URIs, ensuring clients navigate our API as they would a website's pages.

HTTP Methods for CRUD

The mapping CRUD operations to HTTP verbs provides a uniform interface. When we **`GET /tasks`**, we request the collection of all tasks; clients receive a JSON array of task objects. To create a new task, they **`POST`** a JSON payload to **`/tasks`**; the server assigns a new ID and returns the created resource, often with status **`201 Created`** and a **`Location`** header pointing to **`/tasks/{id}`**.

The update of an existing task uses **`PUT`** or **`PATCH`** on **`/tasks/{id}`**:

- **`PUT`** replaces the entire resource, so clients send full task representations.
- **`PATCH`** applies partial updates, such as marking only the **`completed`** flag.

When a client sends **`DELETE /tasks/{id}`**, we remove the task and respond with **`204 No Content`**, indicating success without a response body. Through this, we make our app API predictable: any developer familiar with REST will immediately recognize how to perform standard operations on our resources.

Designing Consistent URI Structures and Versioning

We must try to craft clear, hierarchical URIs that reflect resource relationships. For example:

```
GET    /api/v1/tasks                    # list or filter tasks
POST   /api/v1/tasks                    # create a new task
GET    /api/v1/tasks/{id}               # retrieve a specific task
PUT    /api/v1/tasks/{id}               # replace an existing task
PATCH  /api/v1/tasks/{id}/status  # update only the status
sub-resource
DELETE /api/v1/tasks/{id}               # delete a task
```

By prefixing with **/api/v1**, we introduce versioning, enabling we to evolve the API without breaking existing clients. When we add new fields or change response formats, we increment to **/api/v2** while maintaining **/api/v1** for backward compatibility. We group related resources—such as **/tasks/{id}/tags** for managing a task's tags—under the parent resource URI.

Handling Representations and Content Negotiation

The REST separates resource identity (the URI) from its representations (JSON, XML, YAML). We choose JSON as the primary media type with **application/json** content-type headers. Our server inspects the **Accept** header on incoming requests: if it includes **application/json**, we respond accordingly. For clients that request XML—unlikely in this context—you could implement **application/xml** support.

Additionally, we include hypermedia links in responses (HATEOAS) to assist clients:


```
{
  "id": 42,
  "description": "Buy milk",
  "completed": false,
  "_links": {
    "self": { "href": "/api/v1/tasks/42" },
    "complete": { "href": "/api/v1/tasks/42/status", "method":
"PATCH" }
  }
```

```
}
```

The embedding links lets clients discover available actions dynamically and fosters a more self-descriptive API.

Status Codes and Error Responses

It's really important to have clear, standardized status codes and error payloads for reliable client-server interactions. When a request succeeds, we return:

- **`200 OK`** with a response body for **`GET`**, **`PUT`**, or **`PATCH`**.
- **`201 Created`** with **`Location`** header after **`POST`**.
- **`204 No Content`** after successful **`DELETE`**.

For error conditions, we respond with:

- **`400 Bad Request`** when the client payload is malformed or missing required fields.
- **`404 Not Found`** when a referenced task ID does not exist.
- **`409 Conflict`** if a duplicate task description is not allowed.
- **`500 Internal Server Error`** for unhandled exceptions.

Each of the above error response includes a JSON body with **`error`** and **`message`** fields, for example:

```
{ "error": "BadRequest", "message": "Task description is
required." }
```

If we standardize our error format, clients can parse and react programmatically. This gives users clear feedback and enables automated retries or user prompts.

Enabling Filtering, Pagination, and Sorting

When clients request **`/tasks`**, the collection may grow large. We support query parameters to help them retrieve manageable subsets:

- *Filtering*: **`/tasks?completed=false&highPriority=true`** returns only matching tasks.
- *Pagination*: **`/tasks?page=2&pageSize=20`** returns the second page of results.
- *Sorting*: **`/tasks?sort=createdTimestamp,desc`** orders tasks by creation time.

On the server side, we parse these parameters and apply them to our data store—whether in-memory or database—using filtering, slicing, and sorting operations. We include pagination metadata in responses:

```
{
```

```
  "meta": { "page": 2, "pageSize": 20, "totalCount": 57 },
  "tasks": [ /* array of task objects */ ]
}
```

The clients thus manage large data sets efficiently and display paginated lists in their UIs.

Designing Endpoint and Route Mapping

Defining Resource Routes

Now here, we begin with choosing Ktor for implementing our app API on Linux. The Ktor's routing DSL lets us declare endpoints in code that mirrors our URI structure. In our **`Application.module()`** function, we configure routes under a versioned prefix:

```
fun Application.module() {
    install(ContentNegotiation) {
        json(Json { prettyPrint = true; ignoreUnknownKeys =
true })
    }
    routing {
        route("/api/v1") {
            route("/tasks") {
                get { /* list or filter */ }
                post { /* create */ }
                route("/{id}") {
                    get    { /* retrieve */ }
                    put    { /* replace */ }
                    patch  { /* partial update */ }
                    delete { /* remove */ }
                }
            }
        }
    }
```

```
}
```

You nest **route** blocks so that every handler lives under **/api/v1/tasks** naturally. Path parameters like **{id}** appear in the block for an individual task. By grouping endpoints this way, we avoid repeated prefixes and keep related handlers adjacent.

Extracting Path and Query Parameters

Within a **get** or **post** handler, we access parameters via **call.parameters** or **call.receive**. For example, to fetch a specific task by its ID:

```
get("/{id}") {
    val id = call.parameters["id"]?.toIntOrNull()
    if (id == null) return@get
call.respond(HttpStatusCode.BadRequest, ErrorResponse("Invalid
ID"))
    val task = taskService.getTask(id) ?: return@get
call.respond(HttpStatusCode.NotFound, ErrorResponse("Task not
found"))
    call.respond(task)
}
```

For filtering and pagination on the collection route, we parse query parameters:

```
get {
    val completed =
call.request.queryParameters["completed"]?.toBooleanStrictOrNu
ll()
    val page      =
call.request.queryParameters["page"]?.toIntOrNull() ?: 1
    val pageSize  =
call.request.queryParameters["pageSize"]?.toIntOrNull() ?: 20
    val tasks     = taskService.findTasks(completed, page,
pageSize)
    call.respond(TaskListResponse(tasks, page, pageSize,
taskService.totalCount(completed)))
}
```

By converting string parameters into typed values with **toBooleanStrictOrNull** or **toIntOrNull**, we guard against invalid inputs and respond appropriately.

Handling Request Bodies

When clients **POST** a new task, we decode the JSON body into a DTO and validate it before mapping to our domain model:

```
post {
    val dto = call.receive<CreateTaskRequest>()
    if (dto.description.isBlank()) {
        return@post call.respond(HttpStatusCode.BadRequest,
ErrorResponse("Description cannot be blank"))
    }
    val task = taskService.createTask(dto.description,
dto.highPriority)
    call.response.headers.append(HttpHeaders.Location,
"/api/v1/tasks/${task.id}")
    call.respond(HttpStatusCode.Created, task)
}
```

For **PUT** or **PATCH**, we similarly **receive<UpdateTaskRequest>()**, apply only the provided fields for **PATCH**, and respond with the updated resource.

Organizing Routes into Feature Modules

As our API grows, we extract routing into separate functions for clarity. In **TasksRoutes.kt**:

```
fun Route.taskRoutes(service: TaskService) {
    route("/tasks") {
        getTasks(service)
        postTask(service)
        route("/{id}") {
            getTask(service)
            putTask(service)
            patchTask(service)
```

```
            deleteTask(service)
        }
    }
}
```

Then in **Application.module()**:

```
routing {
    route("/api/v1") {
        taskRoutes(taskService)
        tagRoutes(taskService)    // future endpoints
    }
}
```

If you break routes into feature modules, each file will be focused on one resource, navigation will be simple, and team ownership will be supported.

Applying Consistent Error and Response Model

Across all handlers, we use a shared response model:

```
@Serializable data class ErrorResponse(val error: String, val
message: String)

@Serializable data class TaskListResponse(
    val tasks: List<Task>, val page: Int, val pageSize: Int,
val totalCount: Int
)
```

Here, you respond uniformly: success payloads with **call.respond(data)**, errors with **call.respond(HttpStatusCode.Xxx, ErrorResponse(...))**. This consistency makes client code simpler, since it can parse every non-2xx response into an **ErrorResponse** and every 2xx into the expected data class.

Integrating Database Operations into APIs

When you're doing something that can't be interrupted, you need a store that's going to be there for you. H2 has an embedded, file-based engine that runs on Linux without extra setup, while

PostgreSQL has more robust production features. Kotlin's Exposed library gives us a typesafe DSL over JDBC, which lets us define schemas and perform CRUD operations inside Kotlin code. We combine Ktor, Exposed, and H2 to wire our REST endpoints directly to persistent storage with minimal boilerplate.

Adding Exposed and H2 Dependencies

In our **build.gradle.kts**, we first include:

```
dependencies {
    implementation("io.ktor:ktor-server-core:2.0.0")
    implementation("io.ktor:ktor-server-netty:2.0.0")
    implementation("org.jetbrains.exposed:exposed-
core:0.41.1")
    implementation("org.jetbrains.exposed:exposed-dao:0.41.1")
    implementation("org.jetbrains.exposed:exposed-
jdbc:0.41.1")
    implementation("com.h2database:h2:2.1.214")
    implementation("ch.qos.logback:logback-classic:1.2.11")
}
```

This setup gives us Ktor, the Exposed ORM modules, and the H2 driver for file-backed persistence.

Defining Tasks Table and Entity

Here, we first create **src/main/kotlin/db/TasksTable.kt** with Exposed's DSL:

```
package db
import org.jetbrains.exposed.dao.id.IntIdTable
object TasksTable : IntIdTable("tasks") {
    val description      = varchar("description", length =
255)
    val highPriority     =
bool("high_priority").default(false)
    val completed        = bool("completed").default(false)
    val createdTimestamp = long("created_timestamp")
```

```
}
```

In our **src/main/kotlin/db/TaskEntity.kt**, we map the rows to Kotlin objects:

```
package db
import org.jetbrains.exposed.dao.IntEntity
import org.jetbrains.exposed.dao.IntEntityClass
import org.jetbrains.exposed.dao.id.EntityID
class TaskEntity(id: EntityID<Int>) : IntEntity(id) {
    companion object : IntEntityClass<TaskEntity>(TasksTable)
    var description      by TasksTable.description
    var highPriority     by TasksTable.highPriority
    var completed        by TasksTable.completed
    var createdTimestamp by TasksTable.createdTimestamp
    fun toDomain() = Task(
        id               = id.value,
        description      = description,
        highPriority     = highPriority,
        completed        = completed,
        createdTimestamp = createdTimestamp
    )
}
```

After this, you convert each **TaskEntity** into our domain **Task** data class via **toDomain()**.

Initializing Database Connection

In our **Application.module()** before **routing**, we connect and create tables:

```
import io.ktor.server.application.*
import org.jetbrains.exposed.sql.Database
import org.jetbrains.exposed.sql.SchemaUtils
import org.jetbrains.exposed.sql.transactions.transaction
```

```
import db.TasksTable
fun Application.module() {
    // H2 file "tasks.db" in app directory, persists across
restarts
    Database.connect(
        url      = "jdbc:h2:file:./tasks;DB_CLOSE_DELAY=-1",
        driver   = "org.h2.Driver",
        user     = "sa",
        password = ""
    )
    // Create the tasks table if it doesn't exist
    transaction {
        SchemaUtils.create(TasksTable)
    }
    // install ContentNegotiation, then routing…
}
```

By running **`SchemaUtils.create(...)`** inside a transaction, we ensure the schema matches our table definitions.

Implementing CRUD in Service Layer

Here, at first, we need to factor the database operations into a **`TaskRepository`** backed by Exposed:

```
package service
import db.TaskEntity
import org.jetbrains.exposed.sql.transactions.transaction
class TaskRepository {
    fun allTasks(): List<Task> = transaction {
        TaskEntity.all().map { it.toDomain() }
    }
    fun findById(id: Int): Task? = transaction {
```

```
        TaskEntity.findById(id)?.toDomain()
    }
    fun addTask(task: Task): Task = transaction {
        TaskEntity.new {
            description      = task.description
            highPriority     = task.highPriority
            completed        = task.completed
            createdTimestamp = task.createdTimestamp
        }.toDomain()
    }
    fun updateTask(id: Int, patch: TaskPatch): Task? =
transaction {
        TaskEntity.findById(id)?.apply {
            patch.description?.let { description = it }
            patch.highPriority?.let { highPriority = it }
            patch.completed?.let { completed = it }
        }?.toDomain()
    }
    fun deleteTask(id: Int): Boolean = transaction {
        TaskEntity.findById(id)?.let {
            it.delete(); true
        } ?: false
    }
}
```

With this, we wrap every call in **`transaction { ... }`** to manage commit and rollback automatically. **`TaskPatch`** is a data class with nullable fields for partial updates.

Wiring Repository into Ktor Routes

In **`Application.module()`**, we then instantiate the repository and inject it into our routing:

```
val repository = TaskRepository()
```

```
routing {
    route("/api/v1/tasks") {
        get {
            call.respond(repository.allTasks())
        }
        post {
            val dto = call.receive<CreateTaskRequest>()
            val created = repository.addTask(
                Task(0, dto.description, dto.highPriority,
false, System.currentTimeMillis())
            )
            call.response.headers.append(HttpHeaders.Location,
"/api/v1/tasks/${created.id}")
            call.respond(HttpStatusCode.Created, created)
        }
        route("/{id}") {
            get {
                val id = call.parameters["id"]?.toIntOrNull()
                val task = id?.let { repository.findById(it) }
                if (task == null)
call.respond(HttpStatusCode.NotFound) else call.respond(task)
            }
            put {
                // replace logic similar to patch
            }
            patch {
                val id = call.parameters["id"]?.toIntOrNull()
?: return@patch call.respond(HttpStatusCode.BadRequest)
                val patch = call.receive<TaskPatch>()
                repository.updateTask(id, patch)
                    ?.let { call.respond(it) }
```

```
                    ?: call.respond(HttpStatusCode.NotFound)
            }
            delete {
                val id = call.parameters["id"]?.toIntOrNull()
?: return@delete call.respond(HttpStatusCode.BadRequest)
                if (repository.deleteTask(id))
call.respond(HttpStatusCode.NoContent)
                else call.respond(HttpStatusCode.NotFound)
            }
        }
    }
}
```

By calling **repository** methods directly, our endpoints now persist tasks to the H2 database, retrieve them, apply updates, and delete records transparently.

With all such glue between HTTP requests and persistent storage, our app's RESTful API achieves durable, reliable operations—clients can trust that tasks survive restarts and that updates reflect immediately in our database.

Endpoint Security and API Communication

Securing Access

The goal is to safely expose our app's API, making sure that only approved clients can perform sensitive operations. Ktor supports a bunch of different authentication mechanisms, like Basic, token-based (JWT), and OAuth2. We'll need to install the authentication feature and configure a JWT provider to require a valid JWT for most endpoints.

```
install(Authentication) {
  jwt("auth-jwt") {
    realm = "task-tracker"
    verifier(JwtConfig.verifier)
    validate { credential ->
```

```
        if
(credential.payload.getClaim("username").asString().isNotBlank
())
            JWTPrincipal(credential.payload)
        else null
      }
    }
}
```

We then wrap protected routes in **authenticate("auth-jwt") { ... }**, so calls to **POST**, **PUT**, **PATCH**, and **DELETE** under **/api/v1/tasks** require a valid token carrying a **username** claim. Inside handlers, we retrieve the user's identity via **call.principal<JWTPrincipal>()** and enforce authorization logic—for example, only allow users to delete their own tasks by matching **principal.payload.getClaim("sub")** to the task's **ownerId**.

Encrypting Traffic with HTTPS and TLS

To prevent eavesdropping on credentials or task data, we deploy our Ktor server behind TLS. On Linux, we generate a certificate—self-signed for development or from a CA for production—and configure Netty's SSL connector in **application.conf** or code as shown below:

```
ktor {
  deployment {
    sslPort = 8443
    keyAlias = "tasktracker"
    keyStorePath = "keystore.jks"
    keyStorePassword = "changeit"
    privateKeyPassword = "changeit"
  }
}
```

The clients then connect via **https://your.domain:8443/api/v1/tasks**, and all JSON exchanges occur over encrypted channels, preventing man-in-the-middle attacks.

Validating and Sanitizing Input

Here, the even authenticated requests can carry malformed or malicious payloads. We validate JSON bodies against our DTO classes—**@Serializable** annotations enforce type correctness—but we also perform business-rule checks: descriptions must be non-empty and under 255 characters; timestamps within reasonable bounds.

So in our POST handler:

```
post("/tasks") {
  authenticate("auth-jwt") {
    val req = call.receive<CreateTaskRequest>()
    if (req.description.isBlank() || req.description.length >
255) {
      return@post call.respond(HttpStatusCode.BadRequest,
ErrorResponse("Invalid description"))
    }
    // …
  }
}
```

You reject invalid data with **400 Bad Request** before persisting anything. We also sanitize string fields to escape HTML or SQL if we later integrate with a template engine or direct SQL queries, preventing injection attacks.

Rate Limiting and Throttling

To guard against DoS attacks or accidental floods—such as a bug runaway loop—you implement simple rate limiting per IP or per user. Ktor doesn't include built-in rate limiting, but we can use an in-memory cache like Caffeine or Redis to track request counts.

So we edit the following in our plugin:

```
intercept(ApplicationCallPipeline.Features) {
  val ip = call.request.origin.remoteHost
  if (!RateLimiter.allowRequest(ip)) {
    call.respond(HttpStatusCode.TooManyRequests,
ErrorResponse("Rate limit exceeded"))
    finish()
  }
```

```
}
```

By checking before routing, we ensure abusive clients receive **`429 Too Many Requests`**, protecting our service's capacity for legitimate users.

Configuring CORS and CSRF Protections

If we serve a browser-based UI from the same server or a separate domain, we enable CORS only for trusted origins:

```
install(CORS) {
  method(HttpMethod.Get); method(HttpMethod.Post)
  header(HttpHeaders.ContentType); allowCredentials = true
  host("app.yourdomain.com", schemes = listOf("https"))
}
```

This prevents arbitrary websites from making authenticated requests on users' behalf. For state-changing requests (**`POST`**, **`PUT`**, **`DELETE`**), we also verify CSRF tokens—sending a secure cookie with the JWT or a custom anti-CSRF header—and validate its presence in a custom header before proceeding.

Logging, Monitoring, and Auditing Calls

The security relies on visibility into who accessed what. We integrate Ktor's CallLogging plugin to record every request path, HTTP method, and authenticated principal:

```
install(CallLogging) {
  level = Level.INFO
  filter { call -> call.request.path().startsWith("/api") }
}
```

Now here, combined with our **`ErrorLogger`**, it produces audit trails showing successful and failed attempts. We forward these logs to a centralized monitoring system or SIEM to detect anomalies—such as repeated 401 responses or spikes in 500 errors—letting we respond swiftly to potential attacks or misconfigurations.

Summary

Overall, we learned very well to define the RESTful resources for tasks under

/api/v1/tasks, mapping CRUD operations to HTTP verbs—**GET** to list or retrieve, **POST** to create, **PUT**/**PATCH** to update, and **DELETE** to remove—ensuring stateless interactions and discoverable URIs. We organized routes with Ktor's DSL, nesting version and resource prefixes, extracting path and query parameters with type-safe parsing, and handling request bodies via **call.receive** into request DTOs.

Next, we then connected these endpoints to persistent storage using Exposed ORM and H2: declaring **TasksTable**, mapping rows to **TaskEntity**, and wrapping database operations inside transactions in a **TaskRepository**. We wired repository methods into Ktor handlers, transparently persisting task creations, reads, updates, and deletions. Finally, we secured our API with JWT authentication—installing Ktor's **Authentication** feature, validating tokens, and protecting sensitive routes—while encrypting traffic over HTTPS, validating and sanitizing input payloads, rate-limiting requests, configuring CORS, and logging calls via **CallLogging** and a centralized **ErrorLogger**. Each of the above measures ensured that only authorized clients could perform operations, data remained confidential in transit, and our service resisted abuse and provided comprehensive audit trails.

CHAPTER 12: BUILDING WEB SERVER WITH KTOR

Chapter Overview

Now, let's dive into the last chapter, where we'll start by learning how to set up a Ktor-based web server for our app. This'll include installing the Ktor and serialization plugins in Gradle, setting up a project with the CLI or IDE, and checking out the directory structure that's been generated. Next, we'll set up the application entry point by defining the embedded Netty engine, installing JSON support via ContentNegotiation, and setting up a basic health-check endpoint.

We will then wire our existing **`TaskService`** into the Ktor module and define clean routing functions for CRUD operations under **`/api/v1/tasks`**, covering path and query parameter parsing, request body handling, status codes, and versioned URIs. After that, we will incorporate middleware plugins—CallLogging for request tracing, StatusPages for unified error handling, and a custom validation feature—to enforce consistent serialization, logging, and input validation across all routes.

Finally, we will write systematic tests using Ktor's **`testApplication`**, an in-memory database for integration tests, and manual cURL or Postman collections to validate our server's behavior under normal and error conditions. By chapter's end, we will have a fully functional, tested, and debuggable Ktor web server that exposes our app's functionality to HTTP clients with clarity and resilience.

Initializing Ktor Project

So far, we've been using command-line interactions, but with the growing demand for responsive HTTP interfaces in modern apps, we need to switch things up. Since Ktor's API is defined as Kotlin DSL, we use clear, type-safe code to define routes, interceptors, and middleware. This code integrates seamlessly with our existing Task Tracker domain classes. Ktor's coroutine support is pretty cool because it lets you have a small thread pool that can handle thousands of connections. This gives you high concurrency and low latency. We've got top-notch support for HTTP/2, WebSockets, and asynchronous client calls, which lets us make real-time updates, efficient streaming, and microservice communication happen. With Ktor, we make sure that our web server's architecture lines up with our know-how with Kotlin. This helps us maintain a consistent, idiomatic, and high-performance codebase.

Configuring Build with Ktor and Serialization Plugins

To bring Ktor into our app project on Linux, we update our Gradle build script. In **`build.gradle.kts`**, we then include the Ktor plugin and JSON support:

```
plugins {
    kotlin("jvm") version "1.8.20"
    application
```

```
    id("io.ktor.plugin") version "2.3.0"
    kotlin("plugin.serialization") version "1.8.20"
}
group = "com.example.tasktracker"
version = "1.0.0"
application {
    mainClass.set("com.example.tasktracker.ApplicationKt")
}
repositories { mavenCentral() }
dependencies {
    implementation("io.ktor:ktor-server-core-jvm:2.3.0")
    implementation("io.ktor:ktor-server-netty-jvm:2.3.0")
    implementation("io.ktor:ktor-server-content-negotiation-jvm:2.3.0")
    implementation("io.ktor:ktor-serialization-kotlinx-json-jvm:2.3.0")
    implementation("ch.qos.logback:logback-classic:1.4.7")
    testImplementation("io.ktor:ktor-server-tests-jvm:2.3.0")
    testImplementation("org.jetbrains.kotlin:kotlin-test-junit:1.8.20")
}
```

After saving, we then run **./gradlew build** to download Ktor modules and verify that JSON serialization support is available. The **application** plugin and Ktor plugin together simplify running and packaging our server.

Generating Project Skeleton

To jumpstart our web server, we scaffold a new Ktor module. With the help of Ktor CLI installed via SDKMAN on Linux, we then execute:

```
ktor generate \
  --name TaskTrackerServer \
  --artifact-id task-tracker-server \
```

```
   --package com.example.tasktracker \
   --engine netty \
   --features ktor-server-content-negotiation,ktor-
serialization-kotlinx-json
```

This produces a directory structure with **Application.kt**, **application.conf**, and Gradle files. If we prefer a graphical flow, IntelliJ IDEA's New Project wizard offers a Ktor template: select Kotlin→Ktor, choose Netty engine, enable JSON feature, set group/artifact, and click "Create." Either approach yields a minimal setup where we focus immediately on implementing our app endpoints.

Now you can see that the Ktor project follows a clear convention:

```
task-tracker-server/
├── build.gradle.kts
├── settings.gradle.kts
├── application.conf
└── src/
    ├── main/
    │   ├── kotlin/
    │   │   └── com/example/tasktracker/
    │   │       └── Application.kt
    │   └── resources/
    │       └── application.conf
    └── test/
        └── kotlin/
```

This above layout separates configuration, code, and resources, guiding we to place routing logic, static assets, and tests in the appropriate locations.

Defining Application Entry Point and JSON Support

To do this, we first open **Application.kt** and replace sample code with our app foundation:

```
package com.example.tasktracker
import io.ktor.server.application.*
import io.ktor.server.engine.*
import io.ktor.server.netty.*
import io.ktor.server.plugins.contentnegotiation.*
import io.ktor.serialization.kotlinx.json.*
```

```
import io.ktor.server.routing.*
fun main() = embeddedServer(
    Netty, port = 8080, host = "0.0.0.0"
) {
    module()
}.start(wait = true)
fun Application.module() {
    install(ContentNegotiation) {
        json()  // kotlinx.serialization
    }
    routing {
        route("/api/v1") {
            get("/health") { call.respondText("OK") }
            // task routes will attach here
        }
    }
}
```

With this, we configured the Netty engine on port 8080, installed the ContentNegotiation plugin with JSON support, and established a versioned base route. This code forms the backbone of our web server, ready to grow as we integrate task-specific routes and middleware.

Writing Initial Tests

With our server code in place, we launch it via:

```
./gradlew run
```

The console logs indicate Netty startup. We verify connectivity by running:

```
curl http://localhost:8080/api/v1/health
```

If we see "OK", then it confirms our pipeline from HTTP to Ktor to Kotlin code. To automate this check, we add a test in **src/test/kotlin**:

```
class ApplicationTest {
```

```
    @Test
    fun testHealthCheck() = testApplication {
        application { module() }
        client.get("/api/v1/health").apply {
            assertEquals(HttpStatusCode.OK, status)
            assertEquals("OK", bodyAsText())
        }
    }
}
```

After executing **./gradlew test**, it ensures that core server functionality remains stable as we extend our API. With Ktor installed, configured, and verified, we have established a coroutine-driven web server ready to host our app's RESTful endpoints.

In upcoming topics, we will define detailed task routes, connect the server to our repository layer, layer in authentication, and introduce real-time features such as WebSockets—transforming our command-line tool into a full-featured service accessible by any HTTP client.

Defining Routing and HTTP Handlers

Wiring TaskService into Ktor

Until now, we have a **TaskService** (or **TaskRepository**) that performs all business logic—loading, saving, creating, updating, and deleting tasks. Now before defining routes, we first instantiate and inject this service into our Ktor module:

```
fun Application.module() {
    install(ContentNegotiation) { json() }
    val taskService = TaskService(TaskRepository())  // or
however we construct it
    routing {
        route("/api/v1") {
            taskRoutes(taskService)
        }
    }
```

```
}
```

With the passing of **taskService** into our routing functions, we keep routing code focused on HTTP concerns, delegating data operations to our service layer.

Organizing Routes in Feature Functions

Now here, rather than writing all handlers inline, we group them in a reusable function. In **TasksRoutes.kt**, declare:

```
fun Route.taskRoutes(service: TaskService) {
    route("/tasks") {
        getAllTasks(service)
        getTaskById(service)
        createTask(service)
        updateTask(service)
        patchTask(service)
        deleteTask(service)
    }
}
```

Each call—**getAllTasks**, **getTaskById**, etc.—is an extension function on **Route** that defines one HTTP handler. This separation keeps each handler isolated and testable.

Implementing GET /tasks and GET /tasks/{id}

To list all tasks or fetch one by ID, we define two handlers:

```
fun Route.getAllTasks(service: TaskService) {
    get {
        val tasks = service.getAllTasks()
        call.respond(HttpStatusCode.OK, tasks)
    }
}
fun Route.getTaskById(service: TaskService) {
    get("/{id}") {
```

```
        val idParam = call.parameters["id"]
        val id = idParam?.toIntOrNull()
        if (id == null) {
            call.respond(HttpStatusCode.BadRequest,
ErrorResponse("BadRequest", "Invalid task ID"))
            return@get
        }
        val task = service.getTask(id)
        if (task == null) {
            call.respond(HttpStatusCode.NotFound,
ErrorResponse("NotFound", "Task $id not found"))
        } else {
            call.respond(HttpStatusCode.OK, task)
        }
    }
}
```

You parse **id** safely, respond **400** on parse failure, **404** if no such task, or **200** with the **Task** object when successful.

Handling POST /tasks to Create Task

We must understand that creating a new task requires a JSON payload. For this, we define a request DTO for clarity:

```
@Serializable
data class CreateTaskRequest(val description: String, val
highPriority: Boolean = false)
```

Then implement:

```
fun Route.createTask(service: TaskService) {
    post {
        val req = try {
            call.receive<CreateTaskRequest>()
```

```
        } catch (e: ContentTransformationException) {
            call.respond(HttpStatusCode.BadRequest,
ErrorResponse("BadRequest", "Malformed JSON"))
            return@post
        }
        if (req.description.isBlank()) {
            call.respond(HttpStatusCode.BadRequest,
ErrorResponse("BadRequest", "Description cannot be blank"))
            return@post
        }
        val newTask = service.createTask(req.description,
req.highPriority)
        call.response.headers.append(HttpHeaders.Location,
"/api/v1/tasks/${newTask.id}")
        call.respond(HttpStatusCode.Created, newTask)
    }
}
```

You catch JSON parsing errors, validate the business rule (non-blank description), then call our service to persist and respond with **`201 Created`**, including a **`Location`** header.

Implementing PUT /tasks/{id} for Full Replacement

A **`PUT`** replaces all updatable fields of a task. We use a DTO mirroring the full model:

```
@Serializable
data class UpdateTaskRequest(val description: String, val
highPriority: Boolean, val completed: Boolean)
```

And the route is as below:

```
fun Route.updateTask(service: TaskService) {
    put("/{id}") {
        val id = call.parameters["id"]?.toIntOrNull()
```

```
            ?: return@put
call.respond(HttpStatusCode.BadRequest,
ErrorResponse("BadRequest", "Invalid ID"))
        val req = try { call.receive<UpdateTaskRequest>() }
                  catch (e: ContentTransformationException) {
                      call.respond(HttpStatusCode.BadRequest,
ErrorResponse("BadRequest", "Malformed JSON"))
                      return@put
                  }
        val updated = service.replaceTask(id, req.description,
req.highPriority, req.completed)
        if (updated == null) {
            call.respond(HttpStatusCode.NotFound,
ErrorResponse("NotFound", "Task $id not found"))
        } else {
            call.respond(HttpStatusCode.OK, updated)
        }
    }
}
```

We then funnel the validation and persistence through our service, handle missing tasks, and return the updated resource on success.

Implementing PATCH /tasks/{id} for Partial Updates

When clients want to modify only a subset of fields, **PATCH** with nullable DTOs works best:

```
@Serializable
data class PatchTaskRequest(val description: String? = null,
val highPriority: Boolean? = null, val completed: Boolean? =
null)
```

Following is the route definition:

```
fun Route.patchTask(service: TaskService) {
    patch("/{id}") {
```

```
        val id = call.parameters["id"]?.toIntOrNull()
            ?: return@patch
call.respond(HttpStatusCode.BadRequest,
ErrorResponse("BadRequest", "Invalid ID"))
        val req = try { call.receive<PatchTaskRequest>() }
                  catch (e: ContentTransformationException) {
                      call.respond(HttpStatusCode.BadRequest,
ErrorResponse("BadRequest", "Malformed JSON"))
                      return@patch
                  }
        val patched = service.patchTask(id, req)
        if (patched == null) {
            call.respond(HttpStatusCode.NotFound,
ErrorResponse("NotFound", "Task $id not found"))
        } else {
            call.respond(HttpStatusCode.OK, patched)
        }
    }
}
```

Our service's **patchTask** method applies only non-null fields, centralizing partial-update logic.

Handling DELETE /tasks/{id}

The deletion of the resources is straightforward as shown below:

```
fun Route.deleteTask(service: TaskService) {
    delete("/{id}") {
        val id = call.parameters["id"]?.toIntOrNull()
            ?: return@delete
call.respond(HttpStatusCode.BadRequest,
ErrorResponse("BadRequest", "Invalid ID"))
        val success = service.deleteTask(id)
        if (success) call.respond(HttpStatusCode.NoContent)
```

```
        else call.respond(HttpStatusCode.NotFound,
ErrorResponse("NotFound", "Task $id not found"))
    }
}
```

You respond **204 No Content** on success, **404** when the task does not exist, and **400** for invalid IDs.

Grouping and Versioning Routes

All task routes live under **/api/v1/tasks**. When we introduce new features—such as bulk operations or WebSockets—you can add sibling routes:

```
route("/api/v1") {
    taskRoutes(service)
    route("/bulk") {
        post("/add") { /* handle bulk-add JSON array */ }
    }
    webSocket("/ws/updates") { /* real-time updates */ }
}
```

By combining endpoints like this, we keep the API surface nice and tidy, making it easy to predict what will happen.

Now that we've set up these routing and handler patterns, our app web server is able to efficiently handle client requests. It can process JSON payloads, validate them, persist them to the database, and return consistent responses. All of this is done through clear, type-safe Kotlin code in Ktor's DSL.

Incorporating Middleware and Essential Plugins

Here at Ktor, we see middleware as first-class plugins that we install into our application pipeline. All the plugins handle requests and responses at specific times—like before routing, after serialization, or on errors—so we can add cross-cutting behavior without messing up our business logic. To do this, we use built-in plugins (ContentNegotiation, CallLogging, StatusPages) along with custom interceptors. These help us validate requests, transform data, and monitor performance. When we organize these concerns as plugins, our routing code can focus on handling Task Tracker operations. Middleware makes sure that formatting, security, and observability are consistent across every endpoint.

JSON Serialization via Content Negotiation

We have witnessed that our Task Tracker exchanges JSON with clients. To parse incoming bodies and serialize responses automatically, we need to install the ContentNegotiation plugin early in our module:

```
fun Application.module() {
    install(ContentNegotiation) {
        json(Json {
            prettyPrint     = true
            ignoreUnknownKeys = true
            encodeDefaults = true
        })
    }
    // other plugins and routing…
}
```

Here, the **prettyPrint** makes responses human-readable during development, the **ignoreUnknownKeys** prevents failures when clients send extra fields, and the **encodeDefaults** includes properties with default values for completeness.

After installing, any handler using **call.receive<MyDto>()** or **call.respond(myData)** automatically applies JSON conversion based on our **@Serializable** data classes.

Capturing Traffic with Call Logging

The visibility into requests and responses is critical for debugging. The CallLogging plugin logs each incoming call with method, path, status, and execution time. To configure, we can do as below:

```
install(CallLogging) {
    level = Level.INFO
    format { call ->
        val status = call.response.status() ?: "Unhandled"
```

```
        val method = call.request.httpMethod.value
        val path   = call.request.uri
        "HTTP $method $path → $status"
    }
    filter { call -> call.request.path().startsWith("/api") }
}
```

- **level** controls log verbosity.
- **format** lets us customize each log line.
- **filter** limits logging to API routes.

With this plugin active, every request to **/api/v1/tasks** appears in our console or log file, helping we trace client interactions in real time.

Apart from this, we can make use of the StatusPages plugin to catch exceptions and map them to HTTP responses as shown below:

```
install(StatusPages) {
    exception<BadRequestException> { call, cause ->
        call.respond(HttpStatusCode.BadRequest,
ErrorResponse("BadRequest", cause.message ?: ""))
    }
    exception<AuthenticationException> { call, _ ->
        call.respond(HttpStatusCode.Unauthorized,
ErrorResponse("Unauthorized", "Invalid credentials"))
    }
    exception<Throwable> { call, cause ->
        ErrorLogger.log(cause, "Unhandled")
        call.respond(HttpStatusCode.InternalServerError,
ErrorResponse("ServerError", "Please try again later"))
    }
}
```

In this, the **exception<T>** binds specific exception types to status codes, and the **Throwable** catch-all ensures no uncaught exception crashes our server. Now, throwing

BadRequestException("Missing field") anywhere in our route automatically returns a **400 Bad Request** with a consistent JSON error body.

Validating Requests with Interceptor Plugin

While Ktor does not impose a dedicated validation framework, we can create a small plugin to validate DTOs immediately after deserialization. Define a custom feature:

```
val RequestValidation =
createApplicationPlugin("RequestValidation") {
  onCallReceive { receiveContext ->
    val body = receiveContext.value
    if (body is Validatable) {
      val errors = body.validate()
      if (errors.isNotEmpty()) {
        throw BadRequestException(errors.joinToString("; "))
      }
    }
  }
}
```

Our DTOs implement a simple interface:

```
interface Validatable {
    fun validate(): List<String>
}
@Serializable
data class CreateTaskRequest(val description: String, val
highPriority: Boolean = false) : Validatable {
    override fun validate() = buildList {
        if (description.isBlank()) add("Description must not
be blank")
        if (description.length > 255) add("Description too
long")
    }
```

```
}
```

We can also install the plugin before routing:

```
install(RequestValidation)
```

Every time Ktor deserializes a body via **call.receive<CreateTaskRequest>()**, our plugin invokes **validate()**. If any errors appear, it throws **BadRequestException**, which StatusPages then converts into a **400** response.

Combining Plugins for Robust Operation

Niw if we put it all together, our **Application.module()** will look like:

```
fun Application.module() {
    install(CallLogging) { /* … */ }
    install(ContentNegotiation) { /* JSON config */ }
    install(StatusPages) { /* error mapping */ }
    install(RequestValidation)
    val taskService = TaskService(TaskRepository())
    routing {
        route("/api/v1") { taskRoutes(taskService) }
    }
}
```

If you layer these middleware plugins, you'll get better observability, enforced data integrity, and simpler route handlers. The result is a Ktor server that's ready for production, and it'll handle Task Tracker operations with clarity and resilience.

Testing and Debugging Ktor Components

Although we're using Ktor's asynchronous pipeline, JSON plugins, and routing DSL, some minor bugs can still slip in. We might run into handlers that never fire because of a misplaced route prefix, JSON serialization failures due to mismatched DTOs, authentication misconfigurations that silently reject valid tokens, or middleware ordering that bypasses our validation. We might also see thread-blocking calls inside coroutines, which could lead to unresponsive endpoints under load. If we list these common problems at the start, we can catch them early in development instead of hunting down rare production bugs.

Unit Testing with TestApplication and TestClient

The Ktor provides **`testApplication { }`** to run our module in a lightweight embedded server and exercise routes directly in memory. So here, we begin by adding testing dependencies in **`build.gradle.kts`**:

```
testImplementation("io.ktor:ktor-server-tests-jvm:2.3.0")
```

Then, we write a test for the health endpoint and task routes:

```
class ApiTest {
    @Test
    fun testHealthEndpoint() = testApplication {
        application { module() }
        client.get("/api/v1/health").apply {
            assertEquals(HttpStatusCode.OK, status)
            assertEquals("OK", bodyAsText())
        }
    }
    @Test
    fun testCreateAndGetTask() = testApplication {
        application { module() }
        val createResponse = client.post("/api/v1/tasks") {
            contentType(ContentType.Application.Json)
            setBody("""{"description":"Test
task","highPriority":true}""")
        }
        assertEquals(HttpStatusCode.Created,
createResponse.status)
        val created =
Json.decodeFromString<Task>(createResponse.bodyAsText())
        val getResponse =
client.get("/api/v1/tasks/${created.id}")
        assertEquals(HttpStatusCode.OK, getResponse.status)
```

```
        val fetched =
Json.decodeFromString<Task>(getResponse.bodyAsText())
        assertEquals("Test task", fetched.description)
    }
}
```

By using **client** inside **testApplication**, we simulate HTTP calls without external dependencies, verifying routing, serialization, status codes, and headers in one place.

Integration Testing with Test Databases

When we connect to a real database via Exposed, we avoid polluting production data by configuring a test database. In our test module:

```
@BeforeTest
fun setupTestDatabase() {
    Database.connect("jdbc:h2:mem:test;DB_CLOSE_DELAY=-1",
driver = "org.h2.Driver")
    transaction { SchemaUtils.create(TasksTable) }
}
@AfterTest
fun cleanup() {
    transaction { SchemaUtils.drop(TasksTable) }
}
```

Within **testApplication {}**, we call **setupTestDatabase()** before invoking **module()**. This ensures that every test runs against a fresh schema, letting we create, update, and delete tasks without side effects.

Debugging with Logging and Breakpoints

When a test or manual request fails unexpectedly, we enable detailed logs. Adjust our **CallLogging** in test environment:

```
install(CallLogging) {
    level = Level.DEBUG
    filter { true }  // log all calls
```

```
}
```

In IntelliJ, we set breakpoints inside route handlers or service methods. We run the server in debug mode (**./gradlew run --debug-jvm** or via IDE), trigger a failing request, and step through the pipeline—observing parameter parsing, plugin interceptors, and service invocations. By inspecting **call.parameters**, **call.receive**, and database queries, we pinpoint mismatches between expectations and runtime behavior.

Verifying Middleware Order and Plugin Effects

The middleware ordering matters: for example, **StatusPages** should install before routing to catch exceptions, while **CallLogging** should come early to log every request. We write tests that deliberately trigger errors—such as sending malformed JSON or invalid credentials—and assert that **StatusPages** returns the proper status code and error format. For instance:

```
@Test
fun testBadJsonReturns400() = testApplication {
    application { module() }
    client.post("/api/v1/tasks") {
        contentType(ContentType.Application.Json)
        setBody("{ invalid json }")
    }.apply {
        assertEquals(HttpStatusCode.BadRequest, status)
        assertTrue(bodyAsText().contains("Malformed JSON"))
    }
}
```

Now here, such tests confirm that our plugin chain runs as intended.

Performance Profiling and Stress Testing

Under load, we may detect slow serialization or blocking calls. We integrate Ktor's **MicrometerMetrics** plugin with a simple in-memory registry:

```
install(MicrometerMetrics) {
    registry = SimpleMeterRegistry()
}
```

We can expose metrics at **/metrics** and use JMeter or **hey** to simulate concurrent requests:

```
hey -n 1000 -c 50 http://localhost:8080/api/v1/tasks
```

You then inspect the response times and throughput. If we see blocking warnings in logs, we locate blocking calls—such as file I/O inside coroutines—and refactor them to **withContext(Dispatchers.IO)** or use nonblocking libraries.

Manual Testing with cURL and Postman Collections

Automated tests catch many issues, yet manual exploration uncovers edge cases. We maintain a Postman collection or a set of cURL scripts:

```
curl -X POST -H "Content-Type:application/json" -d
'{"description":"Fix bug"}' http://localhost:8080/api/v1/tasks

curl http://localhost:8080/api/v1/tasks?page=1&pageSize=5

curl -X PATCH -H "Content-Type:application/json" -d
'{"completed":true}' http://localhost:8080/api/v1/tasks/1
```

By experimenting with invalid IDs, missing fields, or oversized payloads, we validate error messages, status codes, and security constraints.

By combining in-memory unit tests, integration tests against a test database, detailed logging, debug sessions, performance profiling, and manual API exploration, we build confidence that our Ktor-based Task Tracker handles every scenario—normal and error—reliably and efficiently.

Summary

So, we finally reach the end of the book. In this chapter, we set up a Ktor-based web server. We installed its Gradle plugin and JSON serialization, and then we used the Ktor CLI or IntelliJ template to scaffold a project.

We explored the directory layout—**Application.kt**, **application.conf**, Gradle scripts—to understand where to place configuration, code, and tests. We configured the embedded Netty engine on port 8080, installed the ContentNegotiation plugin for kotlinx.serialization, and created a health-check route to verify the server. We organized routing by injecting our **TaskService** into the Ktor module and grouping HTTP handlers into feature functions (**taskRoutes**) that handle **GET**, **POST**, **PUT**, **PATCH**, and **DELETE** under **/api/v1/tasks**. We installed essential middleware—ContentNegotiation for JSON, CallLogging for request tracing, StatusPages for centralized error mapping, and a custom validation plugin—to ensure consistent serialization, logging, error responses, and request validation.

Finally, we wrote automated tests using **`testApplication`**, **`TestClient`**, and an in-memory H2 database to verify route behavior, middleware ordering, and serialization, while using logging and breakpoints for debugging.

Index

A

B

C

D

E

F

G

H

I

J

K

L

M

Thank You

www.ingramcontent.com/pod-product-compliance
Lightning Source LLC
Chambersburg PA
CBHW080212170726
48282CB00030B/1093
* 9 7 8 9 3 4 9 1 7 4 5 9 7 *